hamlyn
QuickCook

hamlyn

QuickCook

Gluten-Free Meals

Recipes by Joy Skipper

Every dish, three ways – you choose!
30 minutes | 20 minutes | 10 minutes

An Hachette UK Company
www.hachette.co.uk

First published in Great Britain in 2014 by Hamlyn,
a division of Octopus Publishing Group Ltd
Endeavour House, 189 Shaftesbury Avenue
London WC2H 8JY
www.octopusbooks.co.uk

ISBN 978-0-600-62684-8

A CIP catalogue record for this book is available from the British Library

Printed and bound in China

10 9 8 7 6 5 4 3 2 1

Both metric and imperial measurements are given for the recipes. Use one set of
measures only, not a mixture of both.

Standard level spoon measurements are used in all recipes
1 tablespoon = 15 ml
1 teaspoon = 5 ml

Ovens should be preheated to the specified temperature. If using a fan-assisted oven,
follow the manufacturer's instructions for adjusting the time and temperature. Grills
should also be preheated.

This book includes dishes made with nuts and nut derivatives. It is advisable for
those with known allergic reactions to nuts and nut derivatives and those who may
be potentially vulnerable to these allergies, such as pregnant and nursing mothers,
invalids, the elderly, babies and children, to avoid dishes made with nuts and nut oils.

It is also prudent to check the labels of preprepared ingredients for the possible
inclusion of nut derivatives.

The Department of Health advises that eggs should not be consumed raw. This book
contains some dishes made with raw or lightly cooked eggs. It is prudent for more
vulnerable people such as pregnant and nursing mothers, invalids, the elderly, babies
and young children to avoid uncooked or lightly cooked dishes made with eggs.

Contents

Introduction

30 20 10 – Quick, Quicker, Quickest

This book offers a new and flexible approach to meal-planning for busy cooks, letting you choose the recipe option that best fits the time you have available. Inside you will find 360 dishes that will inspire and motivate you to get cooking every day of the year. All the recipes take a maximum of 30 minutes to cook. Some take as little as 20 minutes and, amazingly, many take only 10 minutes. With a bit of preparation, you can easily try out one new recipe from this book each night and slowly you will be able to build a wide and exciting portfolio of recipes to suit your needs.

How Does it Work?

Every recipe in the QuickCook series can be cooked one of three ways – a 30-minute version, a 20-minute version or a super-quick and easy 10-minute version. At the beginning of each chapter you'll find recipes listed by time. Choose a dish based on how much time you have and turn to that page.

You'll find the main recipe in the middle of the page accompanied by a beautiful photograph, as well as two time-variation recipes below.

If you enjoy your chosen dish, why not go back and cook the other time-variation options at a later date? So, if you liked the 20-minute Mint-Crusted Lamb Cutlets with Pea Mash, but only have 10 minutes to spare this time around, you'll find a way to cook it using cheat ingredients or clever shortcuts.

If you love the ingredients and flavours of the 10-minute Egg-Filled Mushrooms on Toast, why not try something more substantial, like the 20-minute Poached-Egg Topped Mushroom Soup, or be inspired to make a more elaborate version, like Mushroom and Egg Pizzas? Alternatively, browse through all 360 delicious recipes, find something that catches your eye – then cook the version that fits your time-frame.

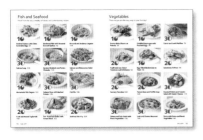

Or, for easy inspiration, turn to the gallery on pages 12–19 to get an instant overview by themes, such as Fish and Seafood or Vegetarian Dishes.

QuickCook Online

To make life easier, you can use the special code on each recipe page to e-mail yourself a recipe card for printing, or email a text-only shopping list to your phone. Go to www.hamlynquickcook.com and enter the recipe code at the bottom of each page.

GLU-SNAX-MUX

QuickCook Gluten-Free Meals

Gluten is a protein composite found in wheat, rye and barley that has the ability to 'hold' foods together and gives dough made from these grains elasticity. Eating a gluten-free diet means avoiding these grains as well as other foods that contain added gluten.

Some people react to eating foods that contain gluten, especially those suffering from coeliac disease, where the gluten causes inflammation in the small intestine. Coeliac disease is a medically diagnosed autoimmune condition in which gluten causes an allergic reaction in the gut, possibly leading to malabsorption of certain nutrients and a range of symptoms including fatigue, weight loss and skin conditions. It has been estimated that as many as one per cent of the population now cannot tolerate gluten, and the rise in coeliac disease has created a huge demand for gluten-free recipes.

However, in recent years eating a gluten-free diet has also become something of a trend, despite the fact that there is no evidence to suggest that eliminating gluten from your diet has any significant benefits for the general population. The only way to be sure of which products or foods affect you adversely is by avoiding them for a few weeks and then reintroducing them one at a time while monitoring your symptoms. If you are on a gluten-free diet to test if your symptoms will improve without gluten, be aware that it may take a while: 3–4 weeks would be a reasonable time to allow.

Approaching the Gluten-Free Diet

When switching to a gluten-free diet, it can initially seem as if there is nothing that you can safely eat. A gluten-free diet rules out all ordinary breads, pasta and many convenience foods, such as gravies, soups and sauces, as gluten is also used as an additive in the manufacture of a wide number of foods, for example as a flavouring or thickening agent in ice cream or ketchup.

According to the Codex Standard for food for special dietary use for persons intolerant to gluten (CODEX STAN11-1979), most, but not all, gluten-sensitive individuals can tolerate oats. Other research suggests that cross-contamination in milling facilities may be to blame for symptoms, or when oats are grown in rotation with wheat. Reading food labels is vital when approaching the gluten-free diet, as there is gluten hidden in many foods, such as soy sauce (use tamari as an alternative), snack foods, meatballs, salad dressing, Worcestershire sauce, dry-roasted nuts, spice mixes, processed meats and even beer (the gluten is in the barley).

On 1 January 2012, new UK legislation on gluten-free foods came into effect, which has led to a change in the way food is labelled:

- Foods labelled 'gluten-free' must contain no more than 20 parts per million gluten.

- Foods labelled 'very low gluten' have between 12 and 100 parts per million gluten.

- 'No gluten-containing ingredients' denotes foods that are made with ingredients that do not contain gluten, and where cross-contamination controls are in place.

Gluten-Free Ingredients

In the past few years the number of gluten-free foods available has increased enormously, with most high street supermarkets stocking a range of gluten-free foods to choose from. The following are suggestions for gluten-free alternatives:

corn (cornflour, cornflakes, corn pasta)
buckwheat (blinis, udon noodles)
gluten-free oats (porridge, oat cakes, oatmeal)
rice (brown, basmati, wild, noodles, crackers, etc.)
millet (flakes, grains, flour, bread)
quinoa (grains, flakes, flour)
potatoes (flour)
kelp noodles
sago and tapioca
pulses (chickpea flour or pasta, soy flour or bread)
nuts (coconut, chestnut, almonds flours)
flax

People who follow a gluten-free diet may have low levels of certain vitamins and other nutrients in their diet, as many grains are enriched with vitamins. Gluten-free food isn't necessarily healthy, though, especially if people are following a gluten-free diet just to be on trend, or in an attempt to lose weight – there is the chance of missing out on important nutrients such as iron, B vitamins (needed for energy) and fibre (important for detoxification). The best sources of iron are meat, poultry, fish, beans and leafy green vegetables, which are all gluten-free.

It may be advisable to visit a nutritionist for advice on how to increase foods that are abundant in these nutrients in your diet and to discuss supplementation, to ensure you are consuming a basic level of nutrients.

Making Your Meals Gluten-Free

Learning to cook gluten-free food is a challenge, but not an impossible one. Once you know which ingredients you are allowed to have and which you should avoid, adapting most recipes is simply a case of trial and error. One school of thought is that when cooking gluten-free food it's best to make only things that were never meant to contain gluten, for example polenta and orange cake, or ground almond chocolate cake, but with so many specialist ingredients now available, most recipes can be adapted to be gluten-free.

Keeping your menu simple is obviously important to start with – go back to basics to get a few staple recipes under your belt before you experiment with more complicated recipes. Fresh meat, fish, vegetables and fruit are all gluten-free and can be used for a whole host of recipes. Fresh eggs, cheese and other dairy products are also safe to use if additive-free (always read labels, as even shop-bought grated cheese sometimes has wheat in it). To ensure there is no cross-contamination in your kitchen, always store your gluten-free foods separately, especially if there is more than one person doing the cooking.

Experiment with different gluten-free flours. There are lots to choose from – rice flour, coconut flour, quinoa flour, almond flour, buckwheat flour – and they all have different textures and tastes, so it may take a while to get used to how they react in cooking and how they taste. You can also buy flour mixes that are gluten-free, and these are probably the best ones to start with.

As with all diets, being organized is the best way to ensure you will stick to the diet. Planning your weekly meals in advance, shopping with a list of foods you are allowed (and reading labels on the foods you buy) and cooking meals from scratch will all help to make life easier and ensure you are eating a balanced diet. This book includes recipes that will help you to stick to the gluten-free diet throughout the day – filling breakfasts, nutritious lunches and tasty family meals – in addition to lots of baked goods and sweet treats to help you realize that you are not missing out on anything at all.

Meaty Treats

Flavour-packed meals to please all meat-lovers

Brunch Bacon Tortilla 56

American Buttermilk Pancakes with Bacon and Maple Syrup 58

Corned Beef Hash 90

Pea and Ham Soup 132

Butternut, Asparagus and Parma Ham Salad 144

Beef Carpaccio and Bean Salad 150

Peppered Steak and Red Onion Salad 154

Roast Pork Chops with Apple and Celery Salad 164

Mint-Crusted Lamb Cutlets with Pea Mash 194

Sausage and Onion Roast with Mustard Mash 210

Cheat's Pancetta and Broccoli Pizza 212

Grilled Calves' Liver with Sage Lentils 214

Chicken and Duck

Nutricious and delicious poultry dishes for every occasion.

Chicken Salad Wraps 68

Duck and Lettuce Wraps 76

Chicken and Vegetable Satay 80

Chicken and Tarragon Pesto Penne 106

Chicken, Red Pepper and Sweet Potato Roast 112

Honey and Mustard Chicken Salad 152

Chicken and Cashew Nut Curry 166

Roast Duck Breast with Plum Sauce 174

Creamy Herb-Stuffed Chicken Breast 192

Mediterranean Olive Chicken 198

Thai Chicken Meatballs with Noodles 206

Chicken en Papillote with Celeriac Mash 216

Fish and Seafood

Fresh from the sea, a medley of classic and contemporary recipes.

Smoked Salmon with Chive Scrambled Egg 28

Mackerel Pâté with Steamed Broccoli Quinoa 92

Broccoli and Anchovy Linguine 108

Salmon Soup 124

Smoked Haddock and Potato Chowder 130

Salmon and Watercress Salad 146

Homemade Fish Fingers 162

Salmon Stew with Mashed Potato 170

Fish Pie 186

Crab and Mussel Tagliatelle 190

Pan-Fried Red Mullet with Fennel Mash 202

Seafood Stir-Fry 208

Vegetarian Meals

These recipes are the easy way to your five day!

Boston Baked Beans on Polenta 38

Griddled Asparagus with Poached Eggs 70

Carrot and Lentil Muffins 78

Fusilli with Sun-Dried Tomatoes and Artichokes 82

Egg-Filled Mushrooms on Toast 86

Sweetcorn Fritters 94

Savoury Pancakes 100

Tuscan Bean and Truffle Soup 120

Roasted Potato and Tomato Salad with Goats' Cheese 136

Quinoa and Feta Salad with Roast Vegetables 156

Leek and Cheese Macaroni 168

Pasta with Pesto and Roast Vegetables 196

Spicy Dishes

Add a hint of heat with these sweet and savoury recipes.

Kedgeree 44

Prawns with Spicy Dip 74

Spicy Turkey Burgers with Red Pepper Salsa 84

Spicy Sweet Potato and Red Pepper Soup 128

Sesame Seared Tuna with Spicy Coriander Salad 148

Mackerel Curry 178

Spaghetti Arrabiata with Chilli and Prawns 184

Spicy Lamb Tagine 200

Stir-Fried Mixed Vegetables with Cashew Nuts 218

Baked Apples with Spiced Fruit 236

Spicy Griddled Pineapple 244

Chilli Hot Chocolate 248

Fruity Favourites

Mouthwatering recipes that are packed with seasonal fruit favourites.

Blueberry Pancakes 26

Sweet French Toast with
Berries and Orange Yogurt 32

Breakfast Banana Split 50

Creamy Mango Smoothie 54

Grapefruit and Sea Bass Tacos
98

Quick Watercress, Beetroot
and Orange Salad 138

Sweet Orange Pancakes 224

Coconut and Raspberry
Muffins 228

Fruit-Stuffed Pancakes 250

Date and Amaretti Tiramisu
254

Banoffee Pie 262

Lemon and Turkish Delight
Syllabub 274

Summer Selection

Let the sun shine with these light and refreshing summer options.

Honey Granola 36

Roasted Peppers 64

Salmon Blinis 66

Grilled Sardines with Pan-Fried Lemon Potatoes 88

Barbecued Vegetable Kebabs with Herb Dipping Sauce 96

Salmon Ceviche 102

Chilled Avocado Soup 122

Butter Bean, Tomato and Feta Salad 134

Cheat's Pepper Pizza 172

Amaretti-Stuffed Peaches 240

Eton Mess 256

Lemon and Raspberry Cheesecake Tartlets 278

Winter Classics

Banish cold and grey with hearty winter recipes.

Berry and Coconut Porridge 34

Cheese and Herb Scones 40

Butternut Squash and Chickpea Soup with Potato Rostis 118

Leek and Rocket Soup 126

Tagliatelle with Dolcelatte and Walnut Sauce 176

Spiced Shepherd's Pie 180

Mushroom Risotto 182

Ratatouille Pizza 204

Caramelized Pears with Salted Caramel Sauce 230

Rhubarb Fool 232

Blueberry and Date Mousse 238

Blackberry and Apple Crumbles 252

QuickCook
Breakfast and Brunch

Recipes listed by cooking time

30

20

10

1⏲ Muesli

Serves 4

200 g (7 oz) rolled oats
50 g (2 oz) dried cranberries
50 g (2 oz) dried apricots,
  chopped
50 g (2 oz) dates, chopped
50 g (2 oz) pecan nuts, chopped
50 g (2 oz) Brazil nuts, chopped
3–4 tablespoons seeds
  (sunflower, pumpkin and
  sesame)

To serve

milk
natural yogurt
fresh fruit

- Mix together all the dry ingredients.
- Divide between 4 bowls and serve with milk, yogurt and fresh fruit.

2⏲ Muesli Bars

In a saucepan, melt 200 g (7 oz) unsalted butter with 200 g (7 oz) dark muscovado sugar and 2 teaspoons clear honey. Stir in 500 g (1 lb) muesli, 2 tablespoons chopped pecans and 100 g (3½ oz) chopped dried apricots. Spoon into a 23 cm (9 inch) square tin and press down. Cook in a preheated oven, 180°C (350°F), Gas Mark 4, for 15 minutes. When cooked, cut into bars and leave to cool in the tin.

3⏲ Bircher Muesli

Make the muesli as above, then place in a bowl and stir in 2 grated apples (with skin) and pour over enough milk, orange or apple juice just to cover. Leave to soak for 20 minutes. Serve with natural yogurt and fresh fruit.

Blueberry Pancakes

Serves 4

125 g (4 oz) self-raising
gluten-free flour
1 teaspoon gluten-free baking
powder
1 egg
150 ml (¼ pint) soya milk
25 g (1 oz) unsalted butter, melted
100 g (3½ oz) blueberries
1 tablespoon olive oil

To serve

crème fraîche
maple syrup

- In a large bowl mix together the flour and baking powder.

- Whisk together the egg and milk and whisk into the flour until smooth.

- Whisk in the melted butter, then stir in 75 g (3 oz) of the blueberries.

- Heat the oil in a frying pan over a medium heat, then spoon tablespoons of the mixture into the pan. Cook for 3–4 minutes until golden underneath then flip over and cook for a further 2–3 minutes. Repeat with the remaining batter.

- Serve with the remaining blueberries, a dollop of crème fraîche and a drizzle of maple syrup.

Blueberry Smoothie

Place 750 ml (1¼ pints) apple juice, 400 g (13 oz) natural yogurt, 3 chopped bananas and 500 g (1 lb) blueberries in a bender and blend until smooth, adding a little milk if too thick. Pour into 4 glasses to serve.

Blueberry Muffins

Sift together 250 g (8 oz) self-raising gluten-free flour, 1 teaspoon gluten-free baking powder and ½ teaspoon bicarbonate of soda. Stir in 75 g (3 oz) sugar. Mix together 55 g (2 oz) melted unsalted butter, 2 eggs and 150 ml (¼ pint) milk, then stir into the flour, adding 125 g (4 oz) blueberries when nearly combined. Line a 12-hole muffin tin with paper cases and spoon in the mixture. Bake in a preheated oven, 200°C (400°F) Gas Mark 6, for 15 minutes until golden and slightly risen. Remove from the tin and cool on a rack.

1 Smoked Salmon with Chive Scrambled Egg

Serves 4

8 eggs

2 tablespoons fromage frais

1 tablespoon chopped chives

125 g (4 oz) smoked salmon,
   cut into strips

salt and pepper

4 slices gluten-free bread,
   toasted and buttered, to serve
   (optional)

- Using a hand whisk, whisk the eggs and fromage frais together with some salt and pepper.

- Heat a saucepan over a medium heat and pour in the egg mixture. Cook for a minute, and then using a spatula, gently push the egg around to allow it all to cook.

- When the egg looks like creamy curds, stir in the chives and smoked salmon and serve immediately on the toast, if using.

---

2 Smoked Salmon Bagels with Poached Eggs and Devilled Tomatoes

Toast 4 halved gluten-free bagels for 2–3 minutes on each side. Spread the bagels with 200 g (7 oz) cream cheese and top with 200 g (7 oz) sliced smoked salmon. Mix 1 tablespoon olive oil with ½ teaspoon ground cumin and ½ teaspoon curry powder. Cut 4 tomatoes in half and brush the cut halves with the spicy oil. Cook under a medium grill for 5–6 minutes. Poach 4 eggs in a frying pan of simmering water for 4-5 minutes. Serve the bagels topped with a poached egg and a sprinkling of chopped chives, with the tomatoes on the side.

---

3 Smoked Salmon Frittata

Thickly slice 500 g (1 lb) new potatoes and cook in boiling water for 8–10 minutes. Drain. Lightly beat 8 large eggs, then stir in 200 g (7 oz) strips of smoked salmon, 2 tablespoons chopped dill, 100 g (3½ oz) petit pois and the potatoes. Season. Heat 2 tablespoons olive oil in a frying pan with an ovenproof handle. Pour in the egg mixture and cook for 10–15 minutes over a low heat until the egg is starting to set. Place under a preheated medium grill and cook for 3–4 minutes, or until the egg is set and the top is golden. Turn out onto a board and cut into wedges to serve.

30 Cocoa, Orange and Pecan Flapjacks

Serves 4

oil, for greasing
100 g (3½ oz) coconut oil
90 g (3¼ oz) blackstrap molasses
20 g (¾ oz) dark muscovado
sugar
25 g (1 oz) agave syrup
250 g (8 oz) rolled oats
50 g (2 oz) pecan nuts, roughly
chopped
50 g (2 oz) cocoa nibs
finely grated rind of 1 orange

- Grease an 18 cm (7 inch) square tin.

- In a large saucepan melt together the coconut oil, molasses, sugar and agave syrup, until the sugar has dissolved.

- Stir in the remaining ingredients and mix well.

- Pour into the prepared tin and level the top.

- Bake in a preheated oven, 180°C (350°F), Gas Mark 4, for 18–20 minutes, then remove from the oven and cut into 12 squares. Leave to cool in the tin.

 Cocoa, Orange and Pecan Porridge

Place 200 g (7 oz) rolled oats in a saucepan with 600 ml (1 pint) milk and 600 ml (1 pint) water. Bring to the boil, then simmer for 8–9 minutes, stirring from time to time so the porridge doesn't stick to the bottom of the pan. Stir in the finely grated rind of 1 orange, then serve sprinkled with 1 tablespoon cocoa nibs and 1 tablespoon chopped pecans and drizzled with 1 tablespoon clear honey.

 Cocoa, Orange and Pecan Muesli

Lightly toast 50 g (2 oz) pecans and 50 g (2 oz) Brazil nuts for 2–3 minutes, then chop roughly. Mix with 200 g (7 oz) rolled oats, 50 g (2 oz) chopped dried apricots, 50 g (2 oz) chopped prunes, 50 g (2 oz) chopped dates, 50 g (2 oz) cocoa nibs and 2–3 tablespoons pumpkin seeds and sesame seeds. Pour into a bowl, cover with orange juice and leave to stand for 10 minutes. Serve with natural yogurt and fresh fruit.

Sweet French Toast with Berries and Orange Yogurt

Serves 4

100 g (3½ oz) blueberries
100 g (3½ oz) strawberries, hulled
  and quartered
2 oranges
400 g (13 oz) Greek yogurt
2 eggs, beaten
50 g (2 oz) caster sugar
2 tablespoons sesame seeds
pinch of ground cinnamon
25 g (1 oz) unsalted butter
4 slices of gluten-free bread

- Place the blueberries and strawberries in a bowl. Grate the rind of the oranges and reserve, then segment the oranges, catching all the juice. Add the orange segments and the juice to the berries.

- Stir the orange rind into the yogurt and chill.

- Whisk together the eggs, sugar, sesame seeds and ground cinnamon.

- Melt the butter in a frying pan over a medium heat. Dip the slices of bread into the egg mixture, place in the pan and cook for 2–3 minutes on each side, until golden.

- Serve each slice of French toast topped with fruit and a dollop of the yogurt, with the juices poured over.

 Warm Berry Compote and Yogurt Place 125 g (4 oz) raspberries, 125 g (4 oz) blueberries and 200 g (7 oz) hulled and halved strawberries in a small saucepan with 2 tablespoons clear honey and heat through for 6–7 minutes, stirring from time to time. Divide 500 g (1 lb) Greek yogurt between 4 small bowls or glasses and pour over the warm compote. Serve immediately.

 Dried Fruit Compote with Lemon Yogurt Grate the rind of 1 lemon and stir into 400 g (13 oz) Greek yogurt with 1 tablespoon lemon curd. Chill. Place 150 g (5 oz) dried fruits, such as apricots, prunes and cranberries, into a pan with 2 stoned and chopped plums. Add ½ teaspoon ground cinnamon and 300 ml (½ pint) orange juice and simmer for 15–18 minutes over a low heat. Leave to cool for 5 minutes, then serve with the lemon yogurt.

10 Berry and Coconut Porridge

Serves 4

200 g (7 oz) rolled oats
600 ml (1 pint) milk
4 tablespoons natural yogurt
200 g (7 oz) fresh berries –
  raspberries, blueberries and
  hulled strawberries
3 tablespoons desiccated
  coconut, plus extra to scatter
4 tablespoons clear honey

- Place the oats in a saucepan with the milk and 600 ml (1 pint) water. Bring to the boil, then simmer for 8 minutes, until thick and creamy, stirring often.

- Pour into 4 warmed bowls and stir in a swirl of the yogurt.

- Top with the berries and a drizzle of honey, then scatter with desiccated coconut.

2 Berry and Coconut Quinoa

Place 175 g (6 oz) quinoa in a saucepan with 300 ml (½ pint) milk, 100 ml (3½ fl oz) water, 100 g (3½ oz) raspberries and ¼ teaspoon ground cinnamon. Bring to the boil, then simmer for 12–15 minutes until the liquid is absorbed and the quinoa is cooked. Serve topped with 2 chopped bananas and 100 g (3½ oz) blueberries, a sprinkling of desiccated coconut and a drizzle of honey.

3 Berry and Coconut Pancakes

Blitz 55 g (2 oz) desiccated coconut in a food processor for 2–3 minutes then pour into a bowl and mix with 60 g (2½ oz) quinoa flour and 1 teaspoon gluten-free baking powder. Whisk in 1 egg, 150 ml (¼ pint) coconut milk and 3 tablespoons caster sugar, then leave the batter to stand for 10 minutes. Stir in 200 g (7 oz) blueberries. Heat a frying pan over a medium heat and lightly grease with vegetable oil. Pour dessertspoons of the mixture into the pan and cook for 2–3 minutes until set and golden underneath, then flip over and cook for a further 1–2 minutes. Remove from the pan and keep warm while cooking the remaining pancakes. Serve the pancakes on warmed plates, topped with a few more blueberries and a drizzle of honey.

30 Honey Granola

Serves 4

15 g (½ oz) clear honey
15 g (½ oz) maple syrup
1 tablespoon sunflower oil
1 tablespoon warm water
45 g (2 oz) dark muscovado sugar
110 g (4 oz) jumbo oats
55 g (2 oz) whole almonds
30g (1 ¼ oz) whole Brazil nuts, chopped
25 g (1 oz) dried cranberries
25 g (1 oz) desiccated coconut

To serve

natural yogurt
fresh berries

- Whisk together the honey, maple syrup, oil, measurement water and sugar.

- Stir in the remaining ingredients, except the cranberries and coconut, and mix well.

- Place the mixture on a baking sheet and spread evenly. Bake in a preheated oven, 150°C (300°F), Gas Mark 2, for 15 minutes, then add the cranberries and coconut and bake for a further 10 minutes. Remove from the oven and pour onto another baking sheet to cool. Leave to cool completely. Store in an airtight container.

- Serve with natural yogurt and fresh berries.

 ### Cinnamon and Honey Porridge

In a small saucepan, mix together 200 g (7 oz) rolled oats, ½ teaspoon ground cinnamon and 750 ml (1¼ pints) water or milk (whichever you prefer). Cook over a medium heat for 8–9 minutes, stirring occasionally, until the porridge thickens. Serve topped with chopped banana and a drizzle of honey.

 ### Honey-Drizzled Pancakes

Mix together 125 g (4 oz) gluten-free flour and 1 teaspoon gluten-free baking powder. Whisk in 1 egg and 150 ml (¼ pint) soya milk until you have a smooth batter. Whisk in 25 g (1 oz) melted butter. Heat 1 tablespoon olive oil in a frying pan over a medium heat, then spoon tablespoons of the mixture into the pan and cook for 3–4 minutes until golden underneath. Flip over and cook for a further 2–3 minutes on the other side. Repeat with the remaining batter and serve warm, drizzled with honey.

10 Boston Baked Beans on Polenta

Serves 4

2 tablespoons olive oil
2 large onions, chopped
1 teaspoon medium curry powder
75 g (3 oz) raisins
2 x 400 g (13 oz) cans baked
beans
6 tablespoons mango chutney
50 g (2 oz) butter
4 slices of cooked polenta
50 g (2 oz) flaked almonds

- Heat half the oil in a saucepan over a medium heat, add the onions and cook for 2–3 minutes, until beginning to soften. Stir in the curry powder, raisins, baked beans and mango chutney. Cook for 4–5 minutes, stirring occasionally.

- Meanwhile, heat the butter and remaining oil in a frying pan over a medium heat, add the polenta and cook for 1–2 minutes on each side.

- Serve the beans spooned over a slice of polenta, sprinkled with the flaked almonds.

20 Devilled Tomatoes with Cheesy

Polenta Brush 4 polenta slices with a little olive oil and cook under a preheated hot grill for 5 minutes on one side. Turn over, sprinkle with 100 g (3½ oz) grated Cheddar and grill for a further 3–5 minutes. Place 12 halved tomatoes on a large piece of foil, cut side down, and grill for 3–4 minutes. Turn the tomatoes over. Mix 2 tablespoons olive oil with 2 crushed garlic cloves, 2 teaspoons mustard powder, 1 teaspoon curry powder and 1 teaspoon ground cumin and spoon a little of the mixture over each tomato. Grill for a further 3–4 minutes. Spread each slice of polenta with 1 tablespoon mango chutney and top with the devilled tomatoes to serve.

30 Polenta Breakfast Pizza

Bring 1 litre (1¾ pints) water to the boil in a saucepan then slowly pour in 250 g (8 oz) polenta, stirring constantly. Season with salt and pepper and add 2 tablespoons chopped parsley. Cook for a further 8–10 minutes until the polenta is thick. Pour half the mixture out onto a lightly oiled baking sheet and spread into a circle about 1 cm (½ inch) thick. Repeat with the rest of the mixture. Bake in a preheated oven, 200°C (400°F), Gas Mark 6, for 12 minutes. Meanwhile, cook 8 unsmoked streaky bacon rashers under a preheated hot grill for 5–6 minutes, or until crisp, then roughly break into bits. Top each polenta round with 2–3 tablespoons tomato purée or sauce and spread it to within 1 cm (½ inch) of the edge. Divide 8 sliced tomatoes, the bacon bits and 75 g (3 oz) grated Cheddar between the polenta rounds and bake for a further 10–12 minutes, until the cheese is golden and bubbling. Serve hot, cut into wedges.

30 Cheese and Herb Scones

Serves 4

350 g (11½ oz) gluten-free self-raising flour

1 teaspoons gluten-free baking powder

1 teaspoon mustard powder

pinch of cayenne pepper

60 g (2½ oz) unsalted butter

200 g (7 oz) Cheddar cheese, grated

1 tablespoon chopped chives, or herb of your choice

2 large eggs

5–6 tablespoons buttermilk

butter, to serve

- Sift the flour, baking powder, mustard powder and cayenne into a large bowl.

- Rub in the butter until the mixture resembles breadcrumbs. Mix in 175g (6 oz) of the grated cheese and the herbs.

- Beat the eggs with the buttermilk and mix into the flour, making a soft dough – do not over work the dough.

- Turn out onto a lightly floured work surface and roll out to a thickness of 2.5 cm (1 inch). Stamp out 12 scones using a 4–5 cm (2 inch) cutter and place onto a baking sheet.

- Sprinkle the remaining cheese over the scones and bake in a preheated oven, 220°C (425°F), Gas mark 7, for 15 minutes, until risen and golden.

- Serve the scones warm, with butter.

Cheese and Herb Pittas

Toast 4 gluten-free pitta breads under a preheated medium grill for 2–3 minutes on each side. Sprinkle with 400 g (13 oz) grated Cheddar mixed with 4 tablespoons chopped chives and place under a preheated hot grill for 2–3 minutes, until golden and bubbling.

Cheese and Herb Muffins

Mix together 100 g (3½ oz) polenta, 125 g (4 oz) almond flour, 100 g (3½ oz) tapioca flour, 3 teaspoons gluten-free baking powder, ¼ tsp paprika, 100 g (3½ oz) grated Cheddar and 2 tablespoons chopped chives. Mix together 125 ml (4 fl oz) sunflower oil, 2 eggs and 225 ml (7½ fl oz) milk, then mix the liquid into dry ingredients to make a batter. Line a 12-hole muffin tin with paper cases and spoon in the mixture. Sprinkle each one with 5 g (¼ oz) grated Cheddar and bake in a preheated oven, 190°C (375°F), Gas Mark 5, for 17–18 minutes until golden.

20 Huevos Rancheros

Serves 4

2 tablespoons olive oil

1 large onion, diced

2 red peppers, deseeded and diced

2 garlic cloves, crushed

¾ teaspoon dried oregano

400 g (13 oz) can chopped tomatoes

4 eggs

20 g (¾ oz) feta cheese, crumbled

4 toasted gluten-free pitta breads, to serve

- Heat the oil in a frying pan over a medium heat, then add the onion, peppers, garlic and oregano and cook for 5 minutes.

- Add the tomatoes and cook for a further 5 minutes. Pour the tomato mixture into a shallow ovenproof dish and make 4 dips in the mixture.

- Crack the eggs into the dips, sprinkle with the feta and cook under a preheated hot grill for 3–4 minutes.

- Serve with toasted pitta breads.

---

10 Tomatoes, Cheese and Egg on Toast

Poach 4 eggs in a frying pan of simmering water for 4–5 minutes. Meanwhile, toast 4 slices of gluten-free bread. Top each one with a sliced tomato and sprinkle with 150 g (5 oz) grated Cheddar. Place under a preheated hot grill and grill for 2–3 minutes, or until golden and bubbling. Top each slice of toast with a poached egg to serve.

30 Traditional Mexican Huevos

Rancheros Cook 900 g (1¾ lb) peeled and diced potatoes in boiling water for 3–4 minutes. Drain well. Heat 2 tablespoons olive oil in a frying pan and add the potatoes. Cook for 5 minutes until they are crisp and golden, then remove with a slotted spoon. Add 1 chopped onion, 2 chopped garlic cloves and 1 deseeded and diced red chilli to the pan and cook for 2–3 minutes, then add 2 deseeded and sliced red peppers and 4 quartered tomatoes. Return the potatoes to the pan, season to taste, then pour into an ovenproof dish. Make 4 dips and crack an egg into each one. Bake in a preheated oven, 200°C (400°F), Gas Mark 6, for 15–18 minutes until the eggs are just set. Sprinkle with 1 tablespoonful chopped parsley to serve.

30 Kedgeree

Serves 4

500 g (1 lb) smoked haddock
50 g (2 oz) butter
1 onion, chopped
¾ teaspoon curry powder
225 g (7½ oz) basmati rice
4 eggs, hard-boiled, peeled and
   quartered
2 tablespoons chopped parsley
½ lemon

- Place the haddock in a saucepan and cover with 600 ml (1 pint) cold water. Bring to a simmer, cover and cook for 8–10 minutes.

- Drain the fish, reserve the liquid and keep the fish warm.

- Using the same pan, melt the butter, add the onion and cook for 1–2 minutes, until softened. Stir in the curry powder and then the rice.

- Pour in 450 ml (¾ pint) of the reserved fish water, bring to a simmer, cover and cook for 15 minutes or until the rice is tender and the water has been absorbed.

- Skin and flake the fish and stir it into the rice with the quartered eggs.

- Serve sprinkled with chopped parsley and a squeeze of lemon juice.

 Smoked Haddock Pâté

Poach 350 g (11½ oz) smoked haddock fillet in a saucepan of simmering water for 5–6 minutes, drain, skin and place in a blender. Add 2 teaspoons lemon juice, 4 tablespoons natural yogurt, a pinch of cayenne pepper and a dash of Worcestershire sauce. Blend until smooth. Serve in individual ramekins with slices of toasted gluten-free bread.

 Smoked Haddock Rarebit

Poach 4 x 150 g (5 oz) smoked haddock fillets in 300 ml (½ pint) simmering milk for 5–6 minutes. Drain and place on a baking sheet. Poach 4 eggs in a frying pan of simmering water for 4–5 minutes, then keep warm. Melt 25 g (1 oz) butter in a saucepan over a medium heat and stir in 50 g (2 oz) plain gluten-free flour. Cook for 1 minute, then slowly pour in 100 ml (3½ fl oz) beer, stirring constantly. Stir in 150 g (5 oz) grated Cheddar, 1 egg yolk, 1 tablespoon Worcestershire sauce, 1 teaspoon mustard and a pinch of cayenne pepper. Cook, stirring constantly, until the cheese melts and the sauce is smooth. Spoon the cheese mixture over the fish and grill under a preheated hot grill for 1–2 minutes, until lightly browned and bubbling. Top each fillet with a poached egg.

Omelette Arnold Bennett

Serves 4

150 ml (5 fl oz) single cream

250 g (8 oz) smoked haddock

4 eggs, separated, plus 2 egg
  whites

10g (¼ oz) butter

10g (¼ oz) Gruyère cheese,
  grated

pepper

crisp green salad, to serve

- Place the cream and pepper to taste in a medium frying pan and add the smoked haddock skinside up. Bring to a simmer.

- Remove the fish with a slotted spoon and skin and flake it. Return the fish to the pan and stir into the cream.

- Whisk together the egg yolks in a bowl. In a separate, grease-free bowl, whisk the egg whites until stiff. Gently fold the egg yolks into the egg whites.

- Melt a little butter in each of 2 omelette pans or small frying pans, then pour half the egg mixture into each. Move it around a little until it starts to cook.

- When the bottom of each omelette is cooked, pour over the creamy haddock mixture and sprinkle with the grated Gruyère. Place under a preheated hot grill and grill for 2–3 minutes until starting to turn golden.

- Halve the omelettes and serve on 4 plates with a crisp green salad. If preferred, cook one omelette in a large frying pan and cut into quarters before serving.

Poached Egg-Topped Smoked Haddock

Haddock Cook 4 x 150 g (5 oz) fillets of smoked haddock in 300 ml (½ pint) simmering milk for 5 minutes. Poach 4 eggs in a frying pan of simmering water for 4–5 minutes. Toast 4 slices of gluten-free bread and spread each slice with 25 g (1 oz) butter and sprinkle with some chopped chives. Place the haddock on the toast and top with a poached egg. Sprinkle with pepper to serve.

Smoked Haddock and Egg Risotto

Melt 50 g (2 oz) butter in a saucepan over a medium heat, add 1 thinly sliced leek and cook for 1–2 minutes. Stir in 300 g (10 oz) Arborio risotto rice and cook, stirring constantly, for 2 minutes. Pour in 700 ml (1¼ pints) fish stock and 250 ml (8 fl oz) milk, bring to the boil and then simmer for 5 minutes. Pour the rice mixture into a buttered ovenproof dish and top with 375 g (12 oz) skinless smoked haddock, cut into large chunks. Cover and bake in a preheated oven, 200°C (400°F), Gas Mark 6, for 15–18 minutes. Meanwhile, poach 4 eggs in a frying pan of simmering water 4–5 minutes and keep warm. Remove the risotto from the oven and stir in 2 tablespoons chopped chives. Divide between 4 shallow bowls and serve topped with a poached egg.

30 Bubble and Squeak Cakes with Poached Eggs

Serves 4

1 kg (2 lb) potatoes, peeled and
  quartered
40 g (1¾ oz) unsalted butter
500 g (1 lb) Brussels sprouts,
  trimmed and halved
50 g (2 oz) plain gluten-free flour
3–4 tablespoons olive oil
4 eggs
salt and pepper
chopped chives, to serve

- Boil the potatoes for 12–15 minutes, until tender, then drain and mash with the butter.

- Meanwhile, cook the sprouts in boiling water for 3–4 minutes, until just tender. Drain and refresh under cold running water.

- Mix the sprouts and potatoes together and season with salt and pepper. Shape the mixture into 8 round cakes and dust with the flour.

- Heat the oil in a frying pan over a medium heat and cook the cakes in 2 batches, for 2–3 minutes on each side, until golden.

- Meanwhile, poach the eggs in a frying pan of simmering water for 4–5 minutes, depending on how you like your eggs.

- Divide the cakes between 4 plates, top each with a poached egg and sprinkle with chopped chives to serve.

1 Mountain Eggs

Heat 4 tablespoons olive oil in a large frying pan. Add 4 large peeled, cooked and chopped potatoes to the pan and cook for 2 minutes. Stir in 200 g (7 oz) chopped smoked ham and make 4 dips in the mixture. Crack one egg into each dip and top with 100 g (3½ oz) grated Emmental. Place under a preheated hot grill for 2–3 minutes until the eggs are set and the cheese is golden and bubbling.

2 Cheesy Bubble and Squeak

Cook 875 g (1¾ lb) peeled and chopped potatoes in a large saucepan of boiling water for 6–8 minutes, then add ½ shredded Savoy cabbage and cook for a further 4 minutes, or until the potatoes are tender. Drain and roughly crush with 50 g (2 oz) unsalted butter. Season with salt and pepper. Heat 2 tablespoons olive oil in a frying pan over a medium heat, add the potato mixture and cook for 6–7 minutes. Sprinkle over 100 g (3½ oz) grated Cheddar and cook under a preheated hot grill for 2 minutes, until bubbling and golden.

 **Breakfast Banana Split**

Serves 4

50 g (2 oz) unsalted butter
2 tablespoons clear honey
4 bananas, cut in half lengthways
2 dessert apples, grated
300 g (10 oz) Greek yogurt
finely grated rind of 1 orange
50 g (2 oz) walnuts, toasted
2 tablespoons flaked almonds,
   toasted
2–3 tablespoons maple syrup

- Melt the butter in a frying pan with the honey until it sizzles.

- Place the bananas in the frying pan, cut side down, and cook for 3–4 minutes, until golden.

- Meanwhile, mix together the grated apple, yogurt and orange rind.

- Spoon the bananas onto 4 warmed plates and top with a large dollop of the yogurt mixture.

- Sprinkle over the nuts, then drizzle with the maple syrup and any juices from the pan to serve.

 Banana and Yogurt Scones

Sift 250 g (8 oz) plain gluten-free flour into a bowl with 1 teaspoon gluten-free baking powder. Rub in 50 g (2 oz) unsalted butter until the mixture resembles fine breadcrumbs. Stir in 50 g (2 oz) caster sugar. Whisk together 1 egg and 150 ml (¼ pint) milk and pour into the flour mixture. Bring the dough together. Using an ice cream scoop, scoop 10 mounds of the dough onto a baking sheet. Bake in a preheated oven, 220°C (425°F), Gas Mark 7, for 12–15 minutes until risen and golden. Serve warm with natural yogurt and sliced bananas.

Banana Buckwheat Pancakes

Place 125 g (4 oz) buckwheat flour in a bowl and whisk in 3 egg yolks, 1 teaspoon clear honey, ¼ teaspoon gluten-free baking powder and a pinch of ground cinnamon. Slowly whisk in 150 ml (¼ pint) milk. In a grease-free bowl, whisk 3 egg whites until soft peaks form and fold into the batter. Heat 1 tablespoon olive oil in a frying pan over a medium heat, add 4 tablespoonfuls of the batter and cook for 2–3 minutes on each side, until golden. Repeat with the remaining batter and keep warm. Meanwhile, in another frying pan melt 50 g (2 oz) butter with 2 tablespoons honey, then stir in 3 sliced bananas and cook for 3–4 minutes, until golden. Spoon the honeyed bananas over the pancakes to serve.

Potato Scones with Cream Cheese and Smoked Salmon

Serves 4

275 g (8 oz) potatoes, peeled and chopped
30 g (1¼ oz) unsalted butter
60 g (2¼ oz) rice flour
pinch of salt
1 teaspoon gluten-free baking powder
1 egg, beaten
2 tablespoons olive oil

To serve

200 g (7 oz) cream cheese
300 g (10 oz) smoked salmon
chopped chives

- Cook the potatoes in a saucepan of boiling water for 10–12 minutes until tender. Drain and mash with the butter until light and fluffy.

- Sift in the flour, salt and baking powder, then add the egg and mix into a dough.

- Turn out onto a lightly floured work surface and roll to a thickness of about 5mm (¼ inch). Cut into 8 wedges and prick all over with a fork.

- Heat the oil in a frying pan over a medium heat and cook the wedges for 4–5 minutes on each side, until golden.

- To serve, spread each scone with a little cream cheese, top with smoked salmon and sprinkle with chopped chives.

---

1 **Bagels with Cream Cheese and Smoked Salmon** Slice 4 gluten-free bagels in half and toast for 2–3 minutes on each side. Spread the toasted bagels with 200 g (7 oz) cream cheese with chives and top with 300 g (10 oz) smoked salmon. Squeeze over the juice of 1 lemon and sprinkle with pepper to serve.

2 **Potato and Smoked Salmon Hash** Cook 625 g (1¼lb) potatoes, peeled and cut into cubes, in a saucepan of boiling water for 10–12 minutes until tender. Meanwhile, place 350 g (11½ oz) salmon fillets under a preheated hot grill and cook for 3–4 minutes on each side. Break the fish into large flakes. Heat 1 tablespoon olive oil in a frying pan over a medium heat, add 1 chopped red onion and 1 deseeded and chopped red pepper and cook for 3–4 minutes. Drain the potatoes, add to the pan and cook for a further for 6–8 minutes, then stir in the flaked salmon. Season and serve.

10 Creamy Mango Smoothie

Serves 4

4 ripe mangoes, peeled and
  stoned
4 tablespoons natural yogurt
1 banana, peeled and chopped
1 litre (1¾ pints) soya milk
clear honey, to sweeten
  (optional)
ice cubes, to serve

- Place all the ingredients except the honey and ice in a blender and blend until smooth.

- Taste for sweetness and add honey, if required, then blend again.

- Pour into 4 tall glasses and serve with ice cubes.

2 Mango with Orange Dressing and Marmalade Yogurt

For the marmalade yogurt, stir 1 tablespoon chunky marmalade into 4 tablespoons Greek yogurt and chill. For the orange dressing, place 6 tablespoons caster sugar and 1 split vanilla pod in a saucepan over a low heat and melt gently. Stir in the grated zest and juice of 4 oranges and 3 tablespoons light muscovado sugar and simmer for 8–9 minutes, until syrupy. Meanwhile, peel 4 mangoes and slice off the cheeks. Heat a griddle pan until smoking hot. Dust the mango cheeks with 2–3 tablespoons icing sugar and chargrill for 2–3 minutes on each side. Serve the mango with a dollop of marmalade yogurt and a drizzle of orange dressing.

3 Marinated Mango Salad

In a bowl, toss together 4 peeled, stoned and chopped mangoes, 2 segmented oranges, 150 g (5 oz) blueberries and 1 tablespoon shredded mint leaves. Mix together 1 tablespoon clear honey, the zest and juice of 2 limes and ¼ teaspoon ground cinnamon. Pour the marinade over the mango salad and leave to marinate at room temperature for 25 minutes. Serve with crème fraîche.

30 Brunch Bacon Tortilla

Serves 4

2 tablespoons olive oil

4 unsmoked streaky bacon rashers

6 large eggs

425 g (14 oz) potatoes, peeled, cooked and diced

150 g (5 oz) baby tomatoes, halved

1 tablespoon chopped parsley

75 g (3 oz) Cheddar cheese, grated

salt and pepper

- Heat 1 tablespoon of the oil in a frying pan over a medium heat, add the bacon and cook for 3–4 minutes. Remove with a slotted spoon.

- Beat the eggs in a large bowl with some salt and pepper, then stir in the bacon, potatoes, tomatoes and parsley.

- Heat the remaining oil in the frying pan over a high heat, pour in the egg mixture and cook for 1–2 minutes, then turn down the temperature.

- Cook for 12–15 minutes, keeping an eye on the edges to make sure the tortilla is not getting too cooked underneath – the top will still be runny.

- Sprinkle over the grated Cheddar and then place the pan under a preheated hot grill and cook for 3–4 minutes, until golden and bubbling.

- To turn out, place a plate on top of the pan and turn upside-down.

- Cut into wedges to serve. This can be eaten hot or cold.

 1 Crispy Bacon with Scrambled Eggs

Grill 4 unsmoked streaky bacon rashers for 6–8 minutes until crisp, then break into pieces. Meanwhile, beat 6 eggs with 4 tablespoons milk and 2 tablespoons chopped chives. Melt a knob of butter in a pan, pour in the egg mixture and cook, stirring, for 5–6 minutes, until nearly set. Spoon onto plates and sprinkle with the bacon bits.

 2 Bacon-Baked Eggs

Melt 50 g (2 oz) butter in a saucepan over a medium heat, add 1 finely diced shallot and 4 diced unsmoked streaky bacon rashers and cook for 1–2 minutes. Add 50 g (2 oz) chopped mushrooms to the pan and cook for a further 3–4 minutes. Stir in 1 teaspoon chopped chives, season with salt and pepper and divide the mushroom mixture between

4 lightly buttered ramekin dishes, making a dip in the centre of each. Break an egg into each dish, top each egg with 1 tablespoon of single cream and season. Stand the dishes in a roasting pan half-filled with hot water and bake in a preheated oven, 180°C (350°F), Gas Mark 4, for 10–15 minutes until the whites are just set and the yolks are still runny.

30 American Buttermilk Pancakes with Bacon and Maple Syrup

Serves 4

1 egg, beaten
175 ml (6 fl oz) buttermilk
15 g (½ oz) butter, melted
50 g (2 oz) tapioca or rice flour
25 g (1 oz) fine cornmeal
1 teaspoon bicarbonate of soda
1 tablespoon sunflower oil
8 unsmoked streaky bacon
  rashers
maple syrup, to serve

- Whisk together the egg, buttermilk and melted butter. Sift in the flour, cornmeal and bicarbonate of soda and mix together gently – do not over mix.

- Heat the oil in a frying pan over a medium heat and pour in 3 large spoonfuls of the batter, to give 3 pancakes. Cook for 2–3 minutes, until bubbles start to appear. Flip the pancakes over gently and cook for a further 1–2 minutes. Remove from the pan and keep warm.

- Repeat with the remaining batter to make a total of 12 pancakes.

  Meanwhile, cook the bacon under a preheated hot grill for 3–4 minutes on each side until crisp.

- Serve the pancakes in stacks of 3 topped with the bacon rashers and drizzled with maple syrup.

---

1 Bacon and Egg Club Sandwich

Toast 12 slices of gluten-free white bread for 2–3 minutes on each side. Meanwhile, grill 8 unsmoked back bacon rashers for 3–4 minutes on each side until crisp and fry 4 eggs to your liking. Spread 4 slices of toast with 2 tablespoons tomato ketchup and top with the bacon. Cover with 4 more slices of toast and top these with 4 sliced tomatoes. Place the eggs on top of the tomatoes and top with the remaining slices of bread to make 4 sandwiches. Secure with cocktail sticks and slice in half to serve.

2 Breakfast Bacon and Sausage Pittas

Cook 4 sausages under a preheated hot grill for 8–10 minutes, turning regularly. Toast 4 gluten-free pitta breads for 2–3 minutes on each side. Grill 8 unsmoked back bacon rashers for 3–4 minutes on each side, until crisp. Spread each pitta with ½ tablespoon tomato ketchup, then top with the bacon, followed by the sausages, cut in half lengthways. Fry 4 eggs to your liking and place on top of the sausages. Sprinkle with 50 g (2 oz) grated Cheddar and place under a hot grill for 2–3 minutes until the cheese is bubbling.

QuickCook

Snacks and Light Lunches

Recipes listed by cooking time

30

20

10

30 Roasted Peppers

Serves 4 (or 8 as a starter)

2 red peppers, halved and deseeded

2 yellow peppers, halved and deseeded

1 small red onion, cut into 8 wedges

2 runner beans, trimmed and cut into small batons

1 courgette, halved and sliced

3 cloves garlic, sliced

2 tablespoons extra virgin olive oil

1 teaspoon cumin seeds

salt and pepper

feta or goats' cheese, to serve

- Place the pepper halves in a roasting tin and divide the other vegetables and the garlic between them.

- Sprinkle with the oil and cumin seeds, season with salt and pepper and bake in a preheated oven, 200°C (400°F), Gas Mark 6, for 25 minutes.

- Crumble over some feta or goats' cheese to serve.

 Red Pepper Hummus

Place a 400 g (13 oz) can chickpeas, rinsed and drained, in a food processor and add the juice of ½ lemon, 2 crushed garlic cloves, 1 teaspoon ground cumin, 2 drained roasted red peppers from a jar, 2 tablespoons tahini paste and 2–3 tablespoons olive oil. Blend until smooth, adding a little more olive oil if you want to loosen the texture. Serve with vegetable crudités.

 Peperonata

Heat 3 tablespoons olive oil in a saucepan over a medium heat, add 2 sliced garlic cloves and 2 sliced onions and cook for 1–2 minutes. Add 4 deseeded and sliced red peppers and cook for a further 10 minutes, then stir in 350 g (11½ oz) chopped ripe tomatoes and cook for a further 8 minutes. Stir in a few torn basil leaves and a sprinkling of pepper to serve.

20 Salmon Blinis

Serves 4

175 g (6 oz) buckwheat flour
2 teaspoons gluten-free baking
  powder
2 eggs
300 ml (½ pint) milk
1 tablespoon olive oil
5 tablespoons crème fraîche
1 tablespoon creamed horseradish
200 g (7 oz) smoked salmon, cut
  into strips
pepper
dill sprigs, to serve

- Sift the flour and baking powder into a bowl, then whisk in the eggs and milk to make a smooth batter.

- Heat the oil in a frying pan over a medium heat and spoon in tablespoons of the batter to make 3–4 cm (1½–1¾ inch) pancakes (the number you can make at one time will depend on the size of your pan). Cook until bubbles appear in the top and the underneath is cooked. Flip over and cook for 1–2 minutes on the other side. Repeat with the remaining batter.

- Mix together the crème fraîche and creamed horseradish and divide the mixture between the pancakes.

- Top each one with smoked salmon and dust with pepper. Serve topped with a dill sprig.

---

10 Salmon Toasts
Toast 4 slices of gluten-free bread for 2–3 minutes on each side. Stir 2 tablespoons chopped chives into 200 g (7 oz) cream cheese, and spread the mixture onto the toast. Top the slices of toast with 200 g (7 oz) smoked salmon strips and sprinkle with pepper to serve.

30 Salmon Terrine
Line a 500 g (1 lb) loaf tin with clingfilm. Arrange 75 g (3 oz) strips of smoked salmon and a few dill sprigs in the bottom of the tin. In a food processor, process 60 g (2½ oz) smoked salmon, 90 g (3¼ oz) poached salmon fillet and 200 g (7 oz) cream cheese until just mixed – do not over process.

Stir in another 50 g (2 oz) chopped smoked salmon, 75 g (3 oz) flaked poached salmon fillet, ½ tablespoon chopped dill and 2 sliced spring onions. Spoon the mixture into the prepared tin and place in the fridge. Toast 4 gluten-free slices of bread or split bagels and serve spread with the terrine.

 # Chicken Salad Wraps

Serves 4

4 ready-made gluten-free
  tortillas
4 tablespoons mayonnaise
4 teaspoons mango chutney
2 carrots, grated
2 cooked chicken breasts,
  shredded
¼ small cabbage, thinly shredded
2 tomatoes, sliced
small handful of coriander leaves
salt and pepper

- Lay the tortillas on the work surface and spread each one with 1 tablespoon of the mayonnaise and 1 tablespoon of the mango chutney.

- Divide the remaining ingredients between the tortillas and season with salt and pepper. Roll up the wraps to serve.

 ### Chicken Club Sandwich

Grill 8 unsmoked streaky bacon rashers under a preheated hot grill for 3–4 minutes on each side until crisp. Toast 12 slices of gluten-free bread for 2–3 minutes on each side. Spread 4 slices of the toast with 2 tablespoons mayonnaise. Top the slices with some shredded iceberg lettuce, 3 sliced tomatoes and the bacon. Spread 4 more slices of toast with 2 tablespoons mango chutney and place on top of the bacon. Cover the mango with 2 sliced cooked chicken breasts and 1 thinly sliced small red onion. Top with the remaining slices of toast and secure each sandwich with 2 cocktail sticks. Slice in half diagonally to serve.

 ### Chicken and Mango Quesadillas

Sprinkle 4 ready-made gluten-free tortillas with 250 g (8 oz) grated Cheddar. Divide 300 g (10 oz) cooked and sliced chicken breast over the cheese. Sprinkle with 1 diced red onion, 2 sliced jalapeno chillies, 1 peeled, stoned and diced mango and a small handful of coriander leaves. Spread 4 more tortillas with 1 tablespoon sour cream each and place them cream side down on the chicken tortillas. Heat ½ tablespoon olive oil in a frying pan over a medium heat, add one of the double tortillas to the pan and cook for 3–4 minutes, until crisp and golden underneath. Carefully turn over and cook for a further 2 minutes. Remove and keep warm, then repeat with the remaining quesadillas. Cut into wedges to serve.

Griddled Asparagus with Poached Eggs

Serves 4

700 g (1 lb 6 oz) asparagus spears
1 tablespoon olive oil
4 eggs
40 g (1¾ oz) Parmesan cheese

- Snap the woody ends off the asparagus spears and discard. Heat a griddle pan until very hot and sprinkle it with the oil.

- Meanwhile, bring a frying pan of water to the boil for the eggs.

- Place the asparagus on the griddle and cook, turning regularly, until slightly charred at the ends.

- Stir the boiling water vigorously then, one at a time, drop the cracked eggs into the centre – the swirling water will help the egg white collect around the yolk and maintain the shape of the egg. Cook for 4–5 minutes then remove with a slotted spoon.

- Serve the asparagus on 4 warmed plates, and top with the poached eggs.

- Using a vegetable peeler, make curly shavings of Parmesan and sprinkle on top of the asparagus.

2 Asparagus Omelette

Heat 1 tablespoon oil in a frying pan, add 6 chopped asparagus spears, 2 sliced spring onions and 3–4 sliced chestnut mushrooms and cook for 5–6 minutes. Whisk together 5 eggs and 4 tablespoons milk and pour into the pan, tipping the pan and moving the egg with a spatula to ensure it all cooks. Sprinkle with 25 g (1 oz) grated Parmesan, then place under a preheated hot grill for 1–2 minutes, until golden. Cut into quarters and serve with a green salad and new potatoes.

3 Asparagus and Poached Egg Salad

Cook 200 g (7 oz) new potatoes in a saucepan of boiling water for 12–15 minutes until tender. Drain. Snap the woody ends off 350 g (11½ oz) asparagus spears and discard. Toss the asparagus and potatoes with 2 tablespoons olive oil. Heat a griddle until very hot and cook the asparagus and potatoes on the griddle for 4–5 minutes, until slightly charred – you may have to do this in batches. Poach 4 eggs in a frying pan of simmering water for 4–5 minutes. Whisk together 3 tablespoons extra virgin olive oil, 1 tablespoon lemon juice, ½ teaspoon mustard and 1 teaspoon clear honey. Toss the dressing with the asparagus, potatoes and a bag of baby salad leaves. Divide between 4 plates and top each one with a poached egg and a sprinkling of Parmesan shavings.

30 Herb Oatcakes

Serves 4

200g (7 oz) rolled oats
3 sprigs rosemary, leaves only
125g (4 oz) gluten-free plain flour
1 teaspoon gluten-free baking
  powder
pinch of salt
75g (3 oz) unsalted butter, cubed
100ml (3½ fl oz) milk

apples and cheese, to serve

- Place the oats and the rosemary in a food processor and process until they start to break down and the mixture resembles breadcrumbs.

- Add the flour, baking powder and salt and blitz again.

- Add the butter and process until it is mixed in, then pour in the milk while the machine is running and process until the dough comes together in a ball.

- Turn out onto a lightly floured work surface and roll out to a thickness of about 4–5 mm (¼ inch). Cut out 20–24 rounds using a 4–5 cm (2 inch) cutter, rerolling as necessary, and place on a baking sheet.

- Bake in a preheated oven, 190°C (375°F), Gas Mark 5, for 12–15 minutes until just starting to turn golden at the edges.

- Cool on a wire rack and serve with cheese and apples. Store in an airtight container.

 Quick Herb Oatcakes
Combine 2 tablespoons olive oil with 4 tablespoons boiling water, then mix in 225 g (7½ oz) oatbran, ¼ teaspoon salt and ½ tablespoon finely chopped rosemary. Work the mixture into a dough and roll out on a work surface sprinkled with oatbran. Cut out 20–24 shapes using a knife or a cutter, and cook in a frying pan over a medium heat for 5 minutes on one side and 4 minutes on the other.

 Smoked Salmon Pâté on Quick Herb Oatcakes Follow the recipe for Quick Herb Oatcakes, substituting the rosemary with dill. Then place 150 g (5 oz) smoked salmon, 2 tablespoons chopped dill, the grated rind and juice of 1 lemon, 2 tablespoons double cream, 5 tablespoons cream cheese and freshly ground black pepper into a blender and blend until smooth. Spread the pâté on the oatcakes and serve topped with snipped chives.

10 Prawns with Spicy Dip

Serves 4

200 g (7 oz) cream cheese
100 g (3½ oz) natural yogurt
1 garlic clove, crushed
2–3 drops lemon juice
¼ teaspoon dried chilli flakes
handful of snipped chives
2 Little Gem lettuces, leaves
  separated
400 g (13 oz) king prawns,
  cooked and peeled
salt and pepper

- To make the spicy dip, mix together the cream cheese, yogurt, garlic, lemon juice, chilli flakes and chives. Season with salt and pepper to taste.

- Arrange the lettuce leaves on 4 small plates and top with the prawns. Serve the dip in a bowl for everyone to share.

2 Spicy Prawn Salad

Heat 2 tablespoons olive oil in a saucepan, add 1 tablespoon dried chilli flakes and 2 crushed garlic cloves and cook for 2 minutes. Add 500 g (1 lb) raw peeled king prawns to the pan and cook for a further 5–6 minutes, until the prawns turn pink and are cooked through. Add a splash of white wine and cook until it has evaporated. Remove from the heat. Toss 75 g (3 oz) rocket leaves in 2 tablespoons olive oil and 1 tablespoon balsamic vinegar. Divide between 4 plates and top with 2 sliced avocados. Spoon over the prawns and serve sprinkled with 1 tablespoon toasted sesame seeds.

3 Spicy Prawn Curry

In a small blender, blend together 2 deseeded red chillies, 1 small chopped red onion, 2 cm (¾ inch) piece of fresh root ginger, peeled and grated, and 2–3 tablespoons water to give a smooth paste. Heat 1 tablespoon vegetable oil in a saucepan, add 1 tablespoon mustard seeds, ½ teaspoon fenugreek seeds and 6 curry leaves and cook until the mustard seeds begin to pop. Stir in the paste and ½ teaspoon turmeric and cook for a further 2–3 minutes, then add 500 g (1 lb) raw peeled tiger or jumbo prawns. Pour in a 400 g (13 oz) can of coconut milk and bring to a simmer. Cook for 6–8 minutes, until the prawns are pink and cooked through. Stir in 2 tablespoons chopped coriander leaves. Serve the curry with cooked basmati rice and a squeeze of lime juice.

 Duck and Lettuce Wraps

Serves 4

6 spring onions

2 cooked duck legs

2 Little Gem lettuces

½ cucumber, cut into thin strips

4–6 tablespoons gluten-free hoisin sauce

2 tablespoons roasted peanuts, roughly chopped

- Cut the spring onions into very long thin strips and place in a bowl of iced water for 4–5 minutes.

- Shred the meat from the duck legs.

- Separate the lettuce leaves and divide the shredded duck between them.

- Garnish each one with cucumber and spring onion, spoon over a little hoisin sauce and sprinkle with the chopped peanuts to serve.

 Duck, Orange and Watercress Salad

Heat 1 tablespoon vegetable oil in a wok over a high heat, add the shredded meat from 2 duck legs, 1 teaspoon Chinese five spice powder and 6 thickly sliced spring onions and stir-fry for 4–5 minutes. Remove from the pan and leave to cool. Whisk together 3 tablespoons extra virgin olive oil, 1 teaspoon sesame oil, 1 tablespoon rice vinegar, 1 teaspoon tamari soy sauce and the finely grated rind and juice of 1 orange. Toss together 2 segmented oranges, 125 g (4 oz) watercress, 125 g (4 oz) sliced radishes, the leaves of 2 chicory bulbs and the cooked spiced duck. Sprinkle over the dressing and 1 tablespoon chopped roasted peanuts.

 Duck Satay with Peanut Sauce

Place 50 g (2 oz) dark muscovado sugar, 100 ml (3½ fl oz) soy sauce, 100 ml (3½ fl oz) sherry, 2 star anise, 1 cinnamon stick, 1 split red chilli and 100 ml (3½ fl oz) water in a saucepan over a medium heat and bring to the boil, then remove from the heat and leave to cool for a few minutes. Pour the marinade over 4 skinless duck breasts and marinate for 15 minutes. Remove the duck from the marinade and pour 100 ml (3½ fl oz) of the marinade into a saucepan with 200 g (7 oz) smooth peanut butter. Cook over a low heat for 5 minutes. Cut the duck breast into strips and thread onto wooden skewers that have been soaked in water to prevent

burning. Mix 2 tablespoons of the peanut sauce with 2 tablespoons olive oil and paint the mixture over the duck satay. Place under a preheated hot grill and cook for 10–12 minutes, turning regularly, until golden. Serve with the remaining peanut sauce.

30 Carrot and Lentil Muffins

Serves 4

75 g (3 oz) red split lentils

275 g (9 oz) plain gluten-free flour

2 tablespoons ground flaxseed

1½ teaspoons gluten-free baking powder

50 g (2 oz) dark muscovado sugar

1 teaspoon ground cinnamon

½ teaspoon ground cloves

3 tablespoons ready-made apple sauce

3 tablespoons clear honey

3 tablespoons sunflower oil

1 egg

1 large carrot, peeled and grated

2–3 tablespoons soya milk (optional)

- Line a 12-hole muffin tin with paper cases.

- Cook the red split lentils in 275 ml (9 fl oz) water for 8 minutes, until soft. Drain.

- Sift the flour, flaxseed and baking powder into a large bowl then stir in the sugar and spices.

- Place the lentils in a food processor with the apple sauce, honey, oil and egg and blend until smooth.

- Pour the wet ingredients into the dry, stirring in the grated carrots when nearly blended. Add the soya milk to loosen the mixture, if needed.

- Spoon into the muffin cases and bake in a preheated oven, 180°C (350°F), Gas Mark 5, for 18–20 minutes until risen and golden. Cool on a rack.

 ### Carrot and Lentil Salad

Blanch 400 g (13 oz) peeled carrots cut into batons in boiling water for 3–4 minutes, then refresh under cold running water. Toss with a 400 g (13 oz) can of green lentils, rinsed and drained, 1 deseeded and diced red pepper, 1 thinly sliced small red onion and 50 g (2 oz) lamb's lettuce. Whisk together 3 tablespoons olive oil, 1 tablespoon white wine vinegar, 1 teaspoon cumin seeds, 1 teaspoon clear honey and ½ teaspoon Dijon mustard and pour over the salad to serve.

 ### Carrot and Lentil Soup

Dry-fry 2 teaspoons cumin seeds and a pinch of dried chilli flakes in a small frying pan for 1 minute. Heat 1 tablespoon olive oil in a saucepan, then add half of the spices, 600 g (1¼ lb) peeled and grated carrots, 150 g (5 oz) red split lentils, 1 litre (1¾ pints) vegetable stock and 125 ml (4 fl oz) milk to the pan and bring to the boil. Simmer for 12–15 minutes, until the lentils are soft and swollen. Using a hand-held blender, blend the soup until smooth. Serve with a drizzle of natural yogurt, a few coriander leaves and the remaining spices sprinkled over the top.

 Chicken and Vegetable Satay

Serves 4

125 ml (4 fl oz) tamari soy sauce

3 tablespoons smooth peanut butter

2 chicken breasts, cut into strips

4 large mushrooms, halved

1 red pepper, deseeded and cut into chunks

1 yellow pepper, deseeded and cut into chunks

1 courgette, halved and sliced

½ Chinese lettuce, shredded

2 carrots, peeled and grated

25 g (1 oz) bean sprouts

small handful of coriander leaves

2 teaspoons sesame oil

juice of 1 lime

2 tablespoons sesame seeds, toasted, to serve

- In a large bowl, mix together the tamari, peanut butter and 2 tablespoons water.

- Toss the chicken and mushrooms, peppers and courgette in the peanut mixture and thread onto 8 satay sticks that have been soaked in water to prevent burning.

- Place under a preheated hot grill and cook for 12–14 minutes, turning regularly, until the chicken is cooked through.

- Meanwhile, toss together the lettuce, grated carrot, bean sprouts and coriander leaves with the sesame oil and lime juice.

- Serve the satay with the salad, sprinkled with toasted sesame seeds.

 Chicken Satay with Satay Sauce

Stir-fry 225 g (7½ oz) peanuts in 100 ml (3½ fl oz) vegetable oil for 1 minute, then blitz until smooth. Fry 2 chopped garlic cloves and 4 chopped shallots for 30 seconds, then add 1 tablespoon tamari soy sauce, 1 teaspoon brown sugar, 1 diced red chilli, 400 ml (14 fl oz) water and the blended peanuts and simmer for 7–8 minutes to thicken. Meanwhile, grill 8 ready-made chicken satay sticks for 3–4 minutes on each side. Stir the juice of 1 lemon into the satay sauce and serve with the chicken.

 Chicken Satay Drumsticks

Mix together 1 tablespoon tamari soy sauce, 1 tablespoon clear honey, 1 teaspoon turmeric, 1 teaspoon ground cumin, 2 crushed garlic cloves, 2 teaspoons grated fresh root ginger, the juice of ½ lime and 1 tablespoon sunflower oil. Pierce 8 chicken drumsticks several times with a sharp knife, place in an ovenproof dish and pour over the marinade. Bake in a preheated oven, 200°C (400°F) Gas Mark 6, for 27–28 minutes. Meanwhile, place 5 tablespoons crunchy peanut butter, 1 teaspoon Thai red curry paste, 125 ml (4 fl oz) coconut milk, 2 teaspoons dark brown sugar and the juice of ½ lime in a small saucepan and bring to a simmer. Cook for 4–5 minutes, until thickened. Serve the chicken wings sprinkled with 1 tablespoon chopped coriander leaves, with the peanut sauce on the side.

Fusilli with Sun-Dried Tomatoes and Artichokes

Serves 4

375 g (12 oz) gluten-free fusilli

2 tablespoons extra virgin olive oil

1 tablespoon balsamic vinegar

½ teaspoon Dijon mustard

½ teaspoon clear honey

1 garlic clove, crushed

10 sun-dried tomatoes, sliced

400 g (13 oz) can artichoke
   hearts, drained and halved

100 g (3½ oz) Parmesan cheese
   shavings

- Cook the fusilli in a pan of boiling water for 9–12 minutes, or according to the pack instructions.

- Whisk together the oil, vinegar, mustard, honey and garlic to make the dressing.

- Drain the pasta and return to the pan with the dressing. Stir in the sun-dried tomatoes and artichoke hearts and warm through.

- Serve in shallow pasta bowls, sprinkled with the Parmesan shavings.

 Artichoke and Sun-Dried Tomato Bruschetta Slice 2 gluten-free baguettes into 16 slices and place on a baking sheet. Drizzle with 2 tablespoons olive oil and toast for 2–3 minutes on each side. Rub one side of each slice with a garlic clove. Top the bruschettta with a 400 g (13 oz) can artichoke hearts, drained and sliced, 12 chopped sun-dried tomatoes and 12 torn slices of Parma ham. Serve sprinkled with 2 tablespoons toasted pine nuts and small basil leaves.

 Tomato, Artichoke and Parma Ham Pizzas Spread 2 large gluten-free pizza bases with a 400 g (13 oz) can of chopped tomatoes, going up to the edges. Top with a 400 g (13 oz) can of artichoke hearts, drained and cut in half, 14 halved sun-dried tomatoes, 6–8 torn basil leaves and 6 slices Parma ham, finishing with 175 g (6 oz) sliced mozzarella. Bake in a preheated oven, 220°C (425°F), Gas Mark 7, until golden and bubbling.

30 Spicy Turkey Burgers with Red Pepper Salsa

Serves 4

400 g (13 oz) minced turkey
2 cm (¾ inch) piece of fresh root ginger, peeled and grated
4 spring onions, finely chopped
1 red chilli, deseeded and finely chopped
1 egg yolk
2 tablespoons chopped coriander leaves
4 Little Gem lettuces

For the salsa

1 red pepper, deseeded and diced
100 g (3½ oz) tomatoes, diced
1 small red onion, finely diced
½ tablespoon chopped parsley
½ tablespoon chopped coriander leaves
1 tablespoon red wine vinegar
½ tablespoon olive oil

- Mix together the minced turkey, ginger, spring onions, chilli, egg yolk and coriander.

- Using wet hands, shape the mixture into 4 burgers.

- Heat a lightly oiled frying pan and cook the burgers for 5–6 minutes on either side, until golden and cooked through.

- Meanwhile, for the salsa, mix together the pepper, tomatoes, onion, parsley, coriander, vinegar and oil.

- Serve the burgers on a bed of lettuce leaves, topped with the salsa.

10 Spiced Turkey-Stuffed Pittas

Toast 4 gluten-free pitta breads for 2–3 minutes on each side. Cut along one edge to open like a pocket. Spread each pitta with ½ tablespoon each mayonnaise and mango chutney. Top with ¼ shredded iceberg lettuce, 4 sliced tomatoes, 350 g (11½ oz) sliced cooked turkey and 1 small thinly sliced red onion. Spoon over ½ tablespoon ready-made salsa and scatter with some chopped coriander to serve.

20 Asian Turkey Salad

Mix together 3 finely sliced shallots with ¼ teaspoon salt and leave to stand for 10 minutes. Whisk together the juice of 1 lime, 2 tablespoons fish sauce, 1 tablespoon rice vinegar, 1 tablespoon caster sugar, 2 crushed garlic cloves and 1 finely diced red chilli. In a large bowl, toss together 350 g (11½ oz) cooked turkey, cut into strips, 400 g (13 oz) finely shredded Chinese cabbage, 1 large peeled and grated carrot, 100 g (3½ oz) bean sprouts and a small handful each of mint and basil. Toss in the shallots and dressing and leave to stand for 5 minutes, then serve sprinkled with 50 g (2 oz) chopped roasted peanuts.

Egg-Filled Mushrooms on Toast

Serves 4

25 g (1 oz) butter
4 eggs, beaten
½ tablespoon chives, chopped
1 tablespoon olive oil
4 portobello mushrooms
4 slices of gluten-free bread,
    toasted
2 tomatoes, chopped
2 spring onions, thinly sliced
salt and pepper

- Melt the butter in a small frying pan. Pour in the eggs and chives, season with salt and pepper and cook for 4–5 minutes, stirring occasionally, until cooked.

- Meanwhile, heat the oil in a frying pan and cook the mushrooms for 3–4 minutes on each side.

- Mix together the tomatoes and spring onions.

- Place the toast on 4 warmed plates and top with the mushrooms, then drizzle over any pan juices.

- Spoon the scrambled egg into the mushrooms and serve sprinkled with the tomato and spring onion mixture.

 Poached Egg-Topped Mushroom Soup Put 25 g (1 oz) dried porcini in a bowl, cover with boiling water and soak for 3–4 minutes. Meanwhile, heat 2 tablespoons olive oil in a large saucepan, add 400 g (13 oz) assorted wild or chestnut mushrooms, 2 crushed garlic cloves, a few thyme leaves and 1 diced red onion and cook for 6–8 minutes. Add the soaked porcini and strained liquid along with 900 ml (1½ pints) vegetable stock and simmer for 6–8 minutes. Blend the soup, using a hand blender, until smooth. Poach 4 eggs in a frying pan of simmering water for 4–5 minutes. Serve the soup in warmed bowls with the eggs and a sprinkling of chopped parsley.

Mushroom and Egg Pizzas Heat 2 tablespoons olive oil in a saucepan over a medium heat, add 1 sliced red onion, 2 sliced garlic cloves and 200 g (7 oz) sliced chestnut mushrooms and cook for 5 minutes. Place 2 large gluten-free pizza bases on baking sheets and spread with 175 g (6 oz) ready-made tomato pizza topping, then sprinkle over 75 g (3 oz) baby spinach leaves and spoon over the mushrooms. Crack 2 eggs on each pizza, one on each half, and top with 75 g (3 oz) grated mozzarella. Bake in a preheated oven, 220°C (425°F) Gas Mark 7, for 22–25 minutes until golden and bubbling. Serve with a salad.

GLU-SNAC-MUX

 # Grilled Sardines with Pan-Fried Lemon Potatoes

Serves 4

625 g (1¼ lb) new potatoes, thickly sliced
1 tablespoon olive oil
12 sardines, cleaned and gutted
grated zest and juice of 1 lemon
2 tablespoons chopped parsley

- Cook the potatoes in boiling water for 12–15 minutes, until tender.

- Heat the oil in a frying pan over a medium heat, add the potatoes and cook for 6–8 minutes, turning regularly, until golden.

- Meanwhile, place the sardines on a grill tray and pour over the lemon juice. Cook the sardines under a preheated hot grill for 2–3 minutes on each side.

- Toss the lemon zest and chopped parsley into the potatoes and serve with the grilled sardines.

 Grilled Sardines on Toast

Cook 8 cleaned and gutted sardines under a preheated hot grill for 2–3 minutes on each side. Meanwhile, toast 4 slices of gluten-free bread. Mix together 3 sliced spring onions, 1 tablespoon chopped parsley and the grated zest of 1 lemon. Season. Place 2 sardines on each slice of toast, spoon over the herb mixture and drizzle with a little olive oil and lemon juice.

 Marinated Sardine Bruschetta

Place 12 butterflied sardines in a shallow dish with the juice and zest of 1 lemon, 4 sliced garlic cloves, 2 torn bay leaves, 1 sliced red chilli and 400 ml (14 fl oz) white wine vinegar. Leave to marinate for 20 minutes. Meanwhile, slice 2 gluten-free baguettes into 12 thick slices, place on a baking sheet and drizzle with 2 tablespoons olive oil. Toast each side for 2–3 minutes, then rub one side of each slice with a garlic clove. Heat a griddle until very hot and cook the sardines for 1 minute on each side. Serve the sardines on the toasted bruschetta with a sprinkling of chopped parsley.

Corned Beef Hash

Serves 4

625 g (1¼ lb) potatoes, peeled
1 tablespoon olive oil
1 onion, chopped
340 g (11½ oz) can corned beef
2 tomatoes, chopped
dash of Worcestershire sauce
2 tablespoons butter or olive oil
4 eggs

- Cook the potatoes in boiling water for 12–14 minutes, until tender.

- Meanwhile, heat the oil in a large frying pan, add the onion and cook for 4–5 minutes.

- Add the corned beef to the pan and cook for a further 2–3 minutes.

- Drain the potatoes and add them to the pan, cooking and lightly crushing them for 1–2 minutes. Stir in the tomatoes and Worcestershire sauce and cook for a further 3–4 minutes.

- Meanwhile, heat the butter or oil in another frying pan and fry the eggs to your liking.

- Serve the corned beef hash topped with a fried egg.

Corned Beef, Egg and Salad Baguette

Slice 4 gluten-free baguettes in half horizontally and toast each piece for 2–3 minutes on each side. Spread the bottom half of each baguette with 1 tablespoon chutney, then top with ¼ shredded iceberg lettuce, 1 sliced hard-boiled egg and one-quarter of a 340 g (11½ oz) can of corned beef, sliced. Sandwich together with the remaining baguettes.

Corned Beef Shepherd's Pie

Cook 625 g (1¼ lb) chopped potatoes in boiling water for 12–15 minutes until tender. Meanwhile, heat 1 tablespoon olive oil in a saucepan over a medium heat, add 1 diced onion, 1 diced celery stick and 1 peeled and diced carrot and fry for 3–4 minutes. Add 350 g (11½ oz) minced beef and brown for 3–4 minutes, then stir in a 340 g (11½ oz) can of corned beef. Pour in 100 ml (3½ fl oz) red wine and simmer for 12–15 minutes. Place in an ovenproof dish. Drain the potatoes and mash with 25 g (1 oz) butter, 100 g (3½ oz) crumbled feta and 1 tablespoon chopped parsley. Spoon over the meat and cook in a preheated oven, 200°C (400°F) Gas Mark 6, for 12 minutes. Serve with steamed Savoy cabbage.

 # Mackerel Pâté with Steamed Broccoli Quinoa

Serves 4

200 g (7 oz) quinoa

250 g (8 oz) broccoli, broken into florets

2 smoked mackerel fillets (about 230 g/7½ oz)

2 spring onions, finely chopped

1 teaspoon horseradish sauce

75g (2¾ oz) soured cream

175 g (6 oz) baby spinach leaves

- Place the quinoa in a saucepan, cover with boiling water and cook for 8–9 minutes, or according to the pack instructions.

- Meanwhile, steam the broccoli florets for 4–5 minutes.

- Skin the mackerel, place in a bowl and break up the flakes with a fork. Add the spring onions, horseradish and soured cream and mix well to form a pâté.

- Drain the quinoa, refresh under cold running water and drain again. Toss together with the broccoli.

- Divide the spinach leaves between 4 plates and top with the quinoa and then the pâté to serve.

 ### Mackerel with Caramelized Red Onion

Heat 1 tablespoon olive oil in a saucepan over a medium heat, add 2 sliced red onions and cook for 2–3 minutes, stirring constantly. Cover and cook for a further 3–4 minutes. Stir in 2 teaspoons balsamic vinegar, then cover and cook for a further 7–8 minutes until the onions are soft and starting to caramelize. Meanwhile, cook 75 g (3 oz) quinoa in boiling water according to the pack instructions. Drain and refresh under running cold water then drain again. Heat ½ tablespoon olive oil in a frying pan, add 4 mackerel fillets, skin side down, and cook for 3–4 minutes, then turn over and cook for a further 3–4 minutes – do not overcook.

Toss together 250 g (8 oz) ready-cooked fresh beetroot wedges, the quinoa, 90 g (3½ oz) rocket leaves and 1 tablespoon salad dressing of your choice. Serve each fillet on a bed of caramelized onions with the salad on the side.

 ### Mackerel with Quinoa Salad

Score 4 whole mackerel 3 times on each side with a knife. Cook 1 teaspoon each of cumin, turmeric and ground coriander in 1 tablespoon olive oil for 1–2 minutes. Brush the spiced oil over the fish. Cook 100 g (3½ oz) quinoa according to the pack instructions. Drain and refresh under cold running water then drain again. Mix together the quinoa, 2 finely sliced spring onions, ½ diced red pepper, 2 diced tomatoes, 2 tablespoons chopped coriander leaves, 1 teaspoon lemon juice, pepper and ½ tablespoon olive oil. Cook the fish under a hot grill for 7–8 minutes on each side until cooked through. Serve with the quinoa salad.

 Sweetcorn Fritters

Serves 4

200 g (7 oz) self-raising
gluten-free flour
1 egg, beaten
150 ml (¼ pint) milk
200 g (7 oz) sweetcorn (drained,
if canned, or thawed, if frozen)
1 tablespoon olive oil
4 eggs
salt and pepper
snipped chives, to serve

- Place the flour in a large bowl and whisk in the egg and milk to make a smooth batter.

- Stir in the sweetcorn and season with salt and pepper.

- Heat the oil in a frying pan over a medium heat, spoon in tablespoons of the batter (the number of fritters you can make at one time will depend on the size of your pan) and cook for 2–3 minutes on each side, until golden. Repeat with the remaining batter.

- Meanwhile, poach the eggs in a frying pan of simmering water for 4–5 minutes.

- Serve a few fritters topped with a poached egg and a sprinkling of chopped chives.

10 Sweetcorn Soup

Heat 2 tablespoons olive oil in a saucepan over a medium heat and add 1 diced onion and 275 g (9 oz) peeled and diced potato. Cook for 1–2 minutes then pour in 1 litre (1¾ pints) hot vegetable stock. Simmer for 5 minutes, until the potato is soft. Stir in 400 g (13 oz) sweetcorn and cook for a further 2 minutes. Stir in 100 ml (3½ fl oz) single cream and, using a hand-held blender, blend half of the soup, leaving the remainder chunky, and mix together. Serve with a sprinkling of chopped chives.

30 Sweetcorn and Potato Frittata

Cook 675 g (1 lb 5 oz) peeled and sliced potatoes in a large saucepan of boiling water for 2–3 minutes until tender. Drain. Heat 2 tablespoons olive oil in a heatproof frying pan, add 1 sliced onion and 1 deseeded and diced red pepper and cook for 2–3 minutes, then remove with a slotted spoon. Beat 8 eggs in a large bowl and stir in the potato mixture, 400 g (13 oz) sweetcorn and 2 tablespoons chopped parsley and season well with salt and pepper. Heat another tablespoon olive oil in the frying pan and gently pour in the egg mixture, moving the ingredients around a little as the egg starts to cook. Continue to cook over a low heat for 12–15 minutes, until the underneath is golden. Sprinkle over 50 g (2 oz) grated Cheddar and place the frying pan under a preheated hot grill for 5–6 minutes, until golden and bubbling. Turn the frittata out onto a board and cut into wedges to serve.

Barbecued Vegetable Kebabs with Herb Dipping Sauce

Serves 4

3 red onions, cut into wedges

2 courgettes, thickly sliced

2 red peppers, deseeded and chopped

1 yellow pepper, deseeded and chopped

4 tablespoons olive oil

1 tablespoon balsamic vinegar

2 tablespoons chopped fresh herbs

salt and pepper

- Thread the vegetables alternately onto 8 bamboo skewers that have been presoaked in cold water to prevent burning.
- Brush the vegetables with 1 tablespoon of the oil and season well with salt and pepper.
- Place the kebabs under a preheated hot grill or barbecue for 12–15 minutes, turning regularly.
- Meanwhile, make the dipping sauce. Mix together the remaining oil, vinegar and herbs in a small bowl.
- Serve the vegetable kebabs with the herb dipping sauce.

Quick Vegetable and Herb Soup

Heat 1 tablespoon olive oil in a saucepan over a medium heat, add 1 large chopped onion, 2 sliced garlic cloves, 3 sliced celery sticks and 300 g (10 oz) finely diced butternut squash and cook for 2–3 minutes. Pour in a 400 g (13 oz) can of chopped tomatoes and 600 ml (1 pint) hot vegetable stock and bring to the boil. Simmer for 7–8 minutes, then stir in 2 tablespoons chopped parsley. Season the soup with salt and pepper to taste and serve.

Roasted Vegetables with Quinoa Herb Salad

In a large roasting tin, toss together 200 g (7 oz) wedges of butternut squash, 2 red onions cut into wedges, 6 trimmed baby leeks, 4 garlic cloves and 2 large peeled and chopped carrots. Sprinkle with some salt and pepper, 2 tablespoons olive oil and 1 tablespoon coriander seeds and roast in a preheated oven, 200°C (400°F), Gas Mark 6, for 25 minutes. Meanwhile, cook 250 g (8 oz) quinoa in a pan of boiling water for 8–9 minutes according to the pack instructions, then drain and refresh under cold running water and drain again. Place in a bowl and mix with ½ diced cucumber, 4 diced tomatoes, the grated rind of 1 lemon, 6 finely sliced spring onions, 20 g (¾ oz) finely chopped parsley and 20 g (¾ oz) finely chopped mint. Stir in 2 tablespoons extra virgin olive oil. Pan-fry 250 g (8 oz) halloumi for 3–4 minutes on each side, until golden. Spoon the quinoa salad onto a large platter and spoon over the roast vegetables. Top with slices of halloumi.

10 Grapefruit and Sea Bass Tacos

Serves 4

500 g (1 lb) sea bass fillet
1 grapefruit, ½ juiced and
   ½ segmented and chopped
1 red chilli, deseeded and thinly
   sliced
4 spring onions, sliced
1 tablespoon chopped coriander
8 taco shells
2 Little Gem lettuces, shredded

- Thinly slice the sea bass fillets and place in a non-metallic bowl with the grapefruit juice and segments, chilli, spring onions and coriander. Mix well.

- Heat the taco shells according to the pack instructions, add half a shredded Little Gem lettuce to the base of each one and then spoon in the sea bass mixture to serve.

2 Pan-Fried Sea Bass with Grapefruit-Dressed Broccoli

Cook 375 g (12 oz) broccoli florets in a pan of boiling water for 2 minutes, then drain. Heat 2 tablespoons olive oil in a frying pan, add the broccoli and cook for 2–3 minutes. Take off the heat and stir in the segments of 2 pink grapefruit. Tip into a bowl and pour over 2 tablespoons grapefruit juice. Season. Score the skin of 4 x 150 g (5 oz) sea bass fillets. Heat 2 tablespoons olive oil in a frying pan, add the fillets, skin side down, and cook for 3–4 minutes on each side. Remove to 4 warmed plates, then add 2 tablespoons capers and 6 roughly chopped anchovies to the pan and cook until they start to crisp. Serve the sea bass fillets on a bed of broccoli and grapefruit, with the capers spooned over the top.

3 Sea Bass and Grapefruit Salad

In a small blender or pestle and mortar, grind together 1 tablespoon paprika, 2 chopped garlic cloves, 1 tablespoon extra virgin olive oil, ½ tablespoon chilli powder, 1 teaspoon dried oregano, ½ teaspoon allspice and 3 tablespoons grapefruit juice. Rub the mixture over 4 x 150 g (5 oz) sea bass fillets and leave to marinate for 15 minutes. Meanwhile, whisk together 5 tablespoons grapefruit juice, 3 tablespoons extra virgin olive oil, 1 tablespoon chopped mint and 1 tablespoon chopped fresh root ginger. Toss together 300 g (10 oz) salad leaves with 2 segmented pink grapefruits, 1 peeled, stoned and chopped mango and 1 peeled, stoned and sliced avocado. Cook the fish under a preheated hot grill for 3–4 minutes on each side. Toss the dressing with the salad, divide between 4 plates and top each one with a sea bass fillet.

 # Savoury Pancakes

Serves 4

500 g (1 lb) carrots, peeled and chopped
400 g (13 oz) can butter beans, rinsed and drained
115 g (3¾ oz) rice flour
1 teaspoon gluten-free baking powder
1 egg
175 ml (6 fl oz) soya milk
2 teaspoons olive oil
50 g (2 oz) walnuts, toasted
2 tablespoons chopped parsley
75 g (3 oz) Cheddar cheese, grated
salt and pepper
crisp green salad, to serve

- Cook the carrots in boiling water for 6–8 minutes, then add the butter beans and cook for a further 2 minutes.

- Meanwhile, in a food processor, blend together the flour, baking powder, egg, milk and 2–3 tablespoons water.

- Heat a lightly oiled frying pan over a medium heat, pour in one-quarter of the batter and cook for 2–3 minutes on each side. Keep warm and repeat with the remaining batter.

- Crush the carrots and butter beans, then stir in the walnuts and parsley. Season with salt and pepper.

- Divide the carrot mixture between the pancakes, placing it in the middle and then folding over each pancake.

- Place the pancakes on a baking sheet, sprinkle with the Cheddar and cook under a preheated hot grill for 3–4 minutes, until golden.

- Serve with a crisp green salad.

 ### Savoury Drop Pancakes

Whisk 2 eggs with 175 g (6 oz) bluckwheat flour, 2 teaspoons gluten-free baking powder and 300 ml (½ pint) milk to give a smooth batter. Heat 1 teaspoon olive oil in a frying pan and pour in 4 tablespoons of the batter to give 4 small pancakes. Cook until small bubbles appear then turn over and cook for a further 1 minute. Repeat with the remaining batter. Top the pancakes with 25 g (1 oz) rocket leaves, 250 g (8 oz) hummus and 2 peeled and grated carrots.

 ### Ratatouille-Stuffed Pancakes

Heat 1 tablespoon olive oil in a saucepan and add 1 diced aubergine, 1 deseeded and chopped red pepper, 1 deseeded and chopped yellow pepper, 1 sliced red onion, 2 sliced courgettes, a 400 g (13 oz) can of chopped tomatoes, 200 ml (7 fl oz) water and ½ teaspoon dried oregano. Bring to a simmer and cook for 20 minutes. Meanwhile, make 4 pancakes as in the recipe above. Divide the ratatouille between the pancakes, roll them up and place them in an ovenproof dish. Pour over 300 ml (½ pint) ready-made cheese sauce, heated according to the pack instructions, and sprinkle over 75 g (3 oz) grated Gruyère, then cook under a preheated hot grill for 3–4 minutes, until golden and bubbling.

30 Salmon Ceviche

Serves 4

450 g (14½ oz) fresh salmon, thinly sliced
juice of 6–8 limes
4 spring onions, finely chopped
2 celery sticks, finely sliced
1 tablespoon fresh coriander, finely chopped
100 g (3½ oz) watercress, to garnish
oatcakes, to serve (optional)

- Place the salmon in a non-metallic bowl and cover with the lime juice. Cover and leave in the fridge for 25 minutes.

- When ready to serve, drain the salmon, add the spring onions, celery and coriander and mix well.

- Garnish with the watercress and serve with oatcakes, if liked.

 Hot-Smoked Salmon Salad

Blanch 200 g (7 oz) trimmed asparagus in a saucepan of boiling water for 1–2 minutes, then drain and refresh under cold running water. Whisk together 3 tablespoons extra virgin olive oil, 1 tablespoon lime juice, 1 teaspoon wholegrain mustard, ½ teaspoon clear honey and 1 deseeded and diced red chilli. In a large bowl toss together 400 g (13 oz) flaked hot-smoked salmon, 4 sliced spring onions, small handful of coriander leaves, 100 g (3½ oz) sliced radishes, 250 g (8 oz) mixed salad leaves, 12 halved baby plum tomatoes, the cooked asparagus and the salad dressing. Serve immediately with lime wedges.

 Salmon and Rice Noodle Stir-Fry

Cook 125 g (4 oz) rice noodles according to the pack instructions. Heat 1 tablespoon olive oil in a wok and cook 400 g (13 oz) sliced salmon fillet with 2 finely chopped garlic cloves for 2–3 minutes. Add 3 chopped tomatoes and 4 sliced spring onions and cook for a further 1–2 minutes. Add 3 tablespoons tamari soy sauce, 1 tablespoon clear honey, the juice of 1 lime and a small handful of coriander leaves. Cook for 1–2 minutes. Divide the noodles between 4 bowls and top with the salmon. Sprinkle over 1 tablespoon sesame seeds and serve garnished with chopped chives.

Bean and Spinach Frittata

Serves 4

750 g (1½ lb) broad beans, fresh or frozen

25 g (1 oz) green beans, trimmed and halved

250 g (8 oz) baby spinach leaves

6 large eggs

small bunch of parsley, chopped

60 g (2½ oz) Manchego cheese, grated

2 tablespoons olive oil

salt and pepper

- Blanch the broad beans in large saucepan of boiling water for 5–6 minutes until tender. Leave to cool a little, then pop the beans out of their skins.

- Blanch the green beans in a saucepan of boiling water for 1–2 minutes, then drain and refresh under cold running water.

- Steam the spinach for 1–2 minutes until wilted. Squeeze out any excess liquid.

- In a large bowl, beat the eggs with some salt and pepper, then stir in the beans, spinach, parsley and one-half of the Manchego.

- Heat the oil in a frying pan and pour in the egg mixture. Turn the heat down to low and cook for 10–12 minutes until cooked underneath. Sprinkle the remaining cheese over the frittata and cook under a preheated medium grill for 2 minutes until golden.

- Turn out onto a board and cut into wedges to serve.

 ### Bean and Spinach Salad

Whisk together 3 tablespoons olive oil and 4 tablespoons lemon juice. Blanch 250 g (8 oz) green beans and 500 g (1 lb) broad beans in a saucepan of boiling water for 5–6 minutes. Drain and refresh under cold running water. Toss the beans with 125 g (4 oz) baby spinach leaves, 3 chopped spring onions and 12 quartered baby plum tomatoes. Sprinkle over 175 g (6 oz) feta and drizzle over the dressing to serve.

 ### Bean and Spinach Stew

Heat 1 tablespoon vegetable oil in a pan over a medium heat add 1 chopped onion and cook for 2–3 minutes. Stir in 3 teaspoons ground cumin and 2 crushed garlic cloves and cook for a further 1–2 minutes. Stir in a 400 g (13 oz) can of chopped tomatoes and 2–3 tablespoons water and cook for 5 minutes. Add a 200 g (7 oz) can of cannellini beans, rinsed and drained, 200 g (7 oz) broad beans, 100 g (3½ oz) trimmed green beans and 1 tablespoon chopped basil and bring to the boil, then simmer for 20 minutes. Stir in 100 g (3½ oz) baby spinach leaves and cook for a further 2–3 minutes.

10 Chicken and Tarragon Pesto Penne

Serves 4

300 g (10 oz) gluten-free penne

125 ml (4 fl oz) olive oil

75 g (3 oz) Parmesan cheese, grated

handful of tarragon leaves

75 g (3 oz) pine nuts, toasted

1 garlic clove, crushed

grated rind and juice of 1 lemon

3 cooked chicken breasts, sliced

100 g (3½ oz) watercress

12 baby tomatoes, quartered

- Cook the penne in a large saucepan of boiling water for 8–9 minutes, or according to the pack instructions. Drain and refresh under cold running water, then toss with 2 tablespoons of the oil.

- Meanwhile, place the Parmesan, tarragon, pine nuts, garlic and lemon rind in a food processor and process for 1 minute. Then, while the machine is running, gradually pour in the remaining olive oil to form the pesto.

- Toss the pesto with the pasta, chicken, watercress, tomatoes and lemon juice, and serve.

2 Chicken and Tarragon Tagliatelle

Toss 4 x 150 g (5 oz) chicken breasts in 2 tablespoons olive oil with 2 tablespoons chopped tarragon and pepper. Cook the chicken breasts under a preheated hot grill for 5–6 minutes on each side until cooked through. Meanwhile, cook 350 g (11½ oz) gluten-free tagliatelle for 9–12 minutes or according to the pack instructions. Heat 1 tablespoon olive oil in a large frying pan over a medium heat, add 4 chopped spring onions and 12 quartered baby tomatoes and cook for 2 minutes. Slice the chicken breasts and add to the pan. Drain the pasta and toss in the pan. Serve sprinkled with 2 tablespoons toasted pine nuts.

3 Chicken and Tarragon Pizza

Spread 175 g (6 oz) ready-made pizza topping on 2 ready-made gluten-free pizza bases. Top each one with 3 sliced tomatoes, 1 deseeded and sliced green pepper, 3 sliced cooked chicken breasts and 150 g (5 oz) sliced mozzarella. Drizzle with 1 tablespoon ready-made pesto and sprinkle with 1 tablespoon chopped tarragon. Bake in a preheated oven, 220°C (425°F), Gas Mark 7, for 25 minutes at until golden and bubbling. Serve with a crisp green salad.

Broccoli and Anchovy Linguine

Serves 4

450g (14½ oz) gluten-free
  linguine
300g (10 oz) broccoli, broken into
  florets
6 tablespoons extra virgin olive oil
1 red chilli, deseeded and finely
  chopped
16 anchovies, chopped

- Cook the pasta in a large saucepan of boiling water for 9 minutes, or according to the pack instructions, adding the broccoli florets after 5 minutes.

- Drain the pasta and broccoli and keep warm.

- Meanwhile, heat the oil in a frying pan over a medium heat, add the chilli and anchovies and stir-fry for 2 minutes.

- Add the pasta and broccoli to the pan, stirring well to coat with the spicy oil. Serve immediately.

 Cheat's Broccoli and Anchovy Pizza

Toast 4 gluten-free pitta breads for 2 minutes on each side. Spread each one with 1½ tablespoons tomato ketchup. Cook 300 g (10 oz) broccoli florets in boiling water for 4–5 minutes, then drain. Heat 1 tablespoon olive oil in a frying pan, add ½ tablespoon chilli flakes and 12 chopped anchovies and cook for 1 minute. Toss the broccoli in the anchovy mixture, then spoon over the pitta breads. Top with 150 g (5 oz) crumbled feta to serve.

Broccoli and Anchovy Pizza

Blanch 300 g (10 oz) broccoli florets in boiling water for 3–4 minutes, then refresh under cold running water and drain. Spread 300 g (10 oz) pizza topping over 2 ready-made gluten-free pizza bases placed on baking sheets. Top with the broccoli, 12 chopped anchovies and 2 sliced garlic cloves. Sprinkle with 100 g (3½ oz) grated mozzarella and bake in a preheated oven, 220°C (425°F), Gas Mark 7, for 20–22 minutes.

 Eggs Florentine

Serves 4

450 g (14½ oz) spinach leaves
15 g (½ oz) butter, melted
pinch of grated nutmeg
4 large eggs
salt and pepper

For the cheese sauce

20 g (¾ oz) butter
20 g (¾ oz) plain gluten-free flour
¼ teaspoon smooth mustard
300 ml (½ pint) milk
75 g (3 oz) strong Cheddar
   cheese, grated

- To make the cheese sauce, melt the butter in a small saucepan then stir in the flour and mustard. Cook, stirring continuously, for 1 minute.

- Pour in the milk gradually, whisking to remove any lumps, then cook over a gentle heat, stirring continuously, until it begins to boil. Turn the heat down to a simmer and stir in two-thirds of the Cheddar.

- Meanwhile, put the spinach in a saucepan with the melted butter and cook for a few minutes. Season with salt and pepper, then add the nutmeg. Place in an ovenproof dish, or divide between 4 individual ovenproof dishes.

- Poach the eggs in a frying pan of simmering water for 4–5 minutes, then drain and place them on top of the spinach.

- Pour over the cheese sauce and sprinkle with the remaining Cheddar. Place under a preheated hot grill and cook until golden and bubbling. Serve immediately.

 Egg, Bacon and Spinach Salad

Grill 4 slices of unsmoked streaky bacon under a hot grill until crisp, then chop roughly. Toss together 150 g (5 oz) spinach leaves with 40 g (1¾ oz) watercress, 4 chopped spring onions, 12 halved baby tomatoes and 2 tablespoons of ready-made salad dressing. Poach 4 eggs in a frying pan of simmering water for 4–5 minutes. Divide the salad between 4 plates and top each one with a poached egg and some crispy bacon.

 Egg and Spinach Omelette

Beat 8 eggs with some salt and pepper and 1 tablespoon crème fraîche. Heat 1 tablespoon sunflower oil in a frying pan over a medium heat, pour one-quarter of the mixture into the pan and swirl it around with a fork, tipping the pan from time to time so all of the egg mixture gets cooked. Sprinkle in 25 g (1 oz) baby spinach leaves and 25 g (1 oz) grated Cheddar and fold over half the omelette to nearly cover the spinach and Cheddar. Cook for a further 1–2 minutes, then remove from the pan and keep warm. Repeat to make 4 omelettes.

30 Chicken, Red Pepper and Sweet Potato Roast

Serves 4

3 red peppers, deseeded and cut into wedges

400 g (13 oz) sweet potatoes, peeled and cut into wedges

2 red onions, cut into wedges

8–10 thyme sprigs

4 garlic cloves

3 tablespoons olive oil

4 chicken breasts

salt and pepper

- Place the peppers, sweet potatoes and onions in a large roasting tin with the thyme and garlic.

- Season well with salt and pepper and drizzle with 2 tablespoons of the oil, then roast in a preheated oven, 200°C (400°F), Gas Mark 6, for 10 minutes.

- Meanwhile, heat the remaining oil in a frying pan or griddle pan over a medium heat and cook the chicken breasts for 4–5 minutes on each side until golden.

- Remove the roasting tin from the oven, toss the vegetables, then nestle the chicken breasts among them and roast for a further 15 minutes, or until the chicken is cooked through.

---

1 Chicken and Red Pepper Salad

Whisk together 3 tablespoons olive oil, 1 tablespoon raspberry vinegar, ½ teaspoon Dijon mustard, 1 crushed garlic clove and ½ teaspoon clear honey. In a large bowl, toss together 2 deseeded and sliced red peppers, 1 thinly sliced small red onion, 12 halved green grapes, 140 g (4¾ oz) watercress, rocket and spinach salad leaves, 3 sliced cooked chicken breasts and 2 tablespoons toasted pumpkin seeds. Toss in the dressing and serve immediately.

2 Chicken, Red Pepper and Sweet Potato Soup

Heat 1 tablespoon olive oil in a frying pan over a medium heat, add 2 diced red onions, 1 deseeded and diced red pepper and 2 crushed garlic cloves and cook for 2–3 minutes, then stir in 500 g (1 lb) peeled and diced sweet potatoes. Add 1 teaspoon ground cumin, then pour in 900 ml (1½ pints) vegetable stock. Simmer for 15 minutes. Using a hand blender, blend until smooth, then season with salt and pepper. Shred 2 cooked chicken breasts and add the meat to the soup, then heat through for 1 minute. Serve with a swirl of natural yogurt.

QuickCook

Soups
and
Salads

Recipes listed by cooking time

10

 # Butternut Squash and Chickpea Soup with Potato Rostis

Serves 4

2 x 400 g (13 oz) cartons ready-made butternut squash soup

400 g (13 oz) can chickpeas, drained

4 medium potatoes, peeled and grated

25 g (1 oz) butter

1 tablespoon olive oil

50 g (2 oz) Manchego cheese, grated

- Heat the butternut squash soup according to the pack instructions, stirring in the chickpeas halfway through the cooking time.

- Meanwhile, squeeze out any moisture from the grated potatoes using a tea towel.

- Heat the butter and oil in a large frying pan. Shape the potato into 4 rough patties and place in the pan. Cook for 3–4 minutes on one side, then turn over, sprinkle with the Manchego and cook for a further 3–4 minutes until golden. Serve the rostis with the soup.

 Creamy Curried Chickpea and Butternut Squash Soup Heat 1 tablespoon oil in a saucepan over a medium heat, add 1 chopped onion and cook for 1–2 minutes. Add 100 g (3½ oz) peeled potatoes, cut into chunks, 400 g (13 oz) can of chickpeas, rinsed and drained, 850 g (1 lb 14 oz) butternut squash, peeled and cut into chunks, and 1 teaspoon mild curry powder, and mix well to coat the vegetables with the spice. Pour in 600 ml (1 pint) vegetable stock and add 50 g (2 oz) chopped creamed coconut, then bring to the boil. Simmer for 12–15 minutes, stirring occasionally, until the potato and pumpkin are soft. Using a hand-held blender, blitz until smooth and creamy. Heat

½ tablespoon olive oil in a small frying pan, add 1 teaspoon cumin seeds and 30 g (1¼ oz) pumpkins seeds and stir-fry for 2–3 minutes until they start changing colour. Serve the pumpkin soup in bowls topped with the spicy pumpkin seeds.

 Butternut Squash and Chickpea Salad Place 425 g (14 oz) butternut squash, peeled and cut into chunks, and 1 red onion cut into wedges in a roasting tray. Season. Sprinkle with 1 tablespoon olive oil and 2–3 thyme springs. Roast in a preheated oven, 200°C (400°F), Gas Mark 6, for 15–20 minutes until tender. Meanwhile, soak 75 g (3 oz) couscous in cold water for 10 minutes, then fluff it up with a fork. Mix in 25 g (1 oz) chopped pecans, a 400 g (13 oz) can chickpeas, rinsed and drained, and 1 teaspoon harissa paste. Gently mix the squash in with the couscous. Divide 50 g (2 oz) rocket leaves between 4 bowls and spoon over the couscous. Whisk together 1 tablespoon olive oil and 2 tablespoons lemon juice and drizzle over.

 # Tuscan Bean and Truffle Soup

Serves 4

2 tablespoons olive oil

1 onion, chopped

2 garlic cloves, sliced

400 g (13 oz) can cannellini beans, rinsed and drained

400 g (13 oz) can butter beans, rinsed and drained

400 g (13 oz) can chopped tomatoes

½ Savoy cabbage, shredded

½ tablespoon chopped fresh rosemary

850 ml (1½ pints) vegetable stock

1 teaspoon truffle oil

salt and pepper

25 g (1 oz) grated Parmesan cheese, to serve

- Heat the oil in a saucepan over a medium heat, add the onion and cook for 1–2 minutes until softened.

- Stir the garlic, cannellini beans and butter beans into the onions and cook for 1 minute.

- Add the tomatoes, cabbage and rosemary to the pan, then pour in the stock and the truffle oil. Mix together well, season and bring to the boil. Simmer for 10–12 minutes, until the cabbage is just cooked.

- Divide the soup between 4 shallow dishes and sprinkle with the Parmesan to serve.

 ### Tuscan Bean and Truffle Salad

Steam 150 g (5 oz) trimmed green beans for 2–3 minutes, then refresh under cold running water and toss together with a 400 g (13 oz) can each of cannellini beans and butter beans, rinsed and drained, 125 g (4 oz) halved baby tomatoes, 4 sliced spring onions and 2 tablespoons chopped parsley. Whisk together 3 tablespoons olive oil, 2 teaspoons truffle oil, 1 tablespoon balsamic vinegar and 1 teaspoon clear honey, pour over the salad and toss to serve.

 ### Sweet Potato and Three-Bean

Truffle Salad Cook 625 g (1¼ lb) peeled and thickly sliced sweet potatoes in a large pan of boiling water for 5 minutes. Drain, then toss with 1 tablespoon olive oil. Heat a griddle until hot and cook the sweet potato slices in batches for 3–4 minutes on each side, until they are slightly caramelized at the edges. Meanwhile, cook 150 g (5 oz) trimmed green beans in boiling water for 2 minutes, then drain and refresh under cold running water. Mix the beans with a 400 g (13 oz) can of butter beans, rinsed and drained, 2 halved baby tomatoes, 1 thinly sliced red onion and ½ cucumber, chopped. Whisk together 3 tablespoons extra virgin olive oil, 1 teaspoon truffle oil, 1 teaspoon Dijon mustard and 1 tablespoon balsamic vinegar. Toss the beans with the dressing and serve the bean salad spooned over the slices of griddled sweet potato.

 # Chilled Avocado Soup

Serves 4

4 large avocados, peeled and
  stoned
juice of 1 lime
½ red chilli, deseeded and diced
900 ml (1½ pints) vegetable
  stock, chilled
2 spring onions, finely sliced
½ red pepper, deseeded and diced
¼ cucumber, diced
1 tablespoon coriander leaves
2 tablespoons olive oil
2 teaspoons lemon juice
2 tablespoons pumpkin seeds,
  toasted
salt and pepper
8 ice cubes, to serve

- Place the avocados, lime juice and chilli in a food processor and blend with the chilled stock until smooth. Season to taste with salt and pepper and chill for 15 minutes.

- Meanwhile, mix together the remaining ingredients.

- Place 2 ice cubes in each of 4 shallow bowls, and pour over the soup.

- Sprinkle over the salsa and serve.

 ### Guacamole Avocado Salad

Mix together 3 peeled, stoned and chopped avocados, 2 chopped tomatoes, 1 diced red chilli, 2 crushed garlic cloves, 1 small bunch of coriander, chopped, the juice of ½ lime and some salt and pepper, then lightly mash together. Toss 250 g (8 oz) mixed salad leaves and ½ sliced cucumber with 2 tablespoons of your favourite salad dressing. Divide the salad leaves between 4 plates and top with the guacamole to serve.

 ### Warm Avocado Salad with Chorizo

Heat 2 tablespoons olive oil in a pan and fry 3 thick slices of gluten-free bread, cut into 2 cm (¾ inch) cubes, until golden. Remove the croûtons from the pan. Add 175 g (6 oz) chorizo to the pan and cook for 3–4 minutes, until it starts releasing its oil, then add 250 g (8 oz) baby tomatoes. Cook for 2–3 minutes, then add 2 tablespoons balsamic vinegar and a pinch of caster sugar. Toss together 175 g (6 oz) mixed salad leaves and 2 peeled, stoned and sliced avocados with the croûtons. Spoon over the chorizo and tomatoes, then drizzle over the juices from the pan and serve immediately.

Salmon Soup

Serves 4

475 g (15 oz) cauliflower, cut into
florets

50 g (2 oz) unsalted butter

1 onion, chopped

1 leek, shredded

625 g (1¼ lb) potatoes, peeled
and diced

275 g (9 oz) swede, peeled and
diced

1.2 litres (2 pints) fish stock

2 tomatoes, chopped

500 g (1 lb) salmon fillet, cut into
large chunks

100 ml (3½ fl oz) double cream

1 teaspoon creamed horseradish

juice of ½ lemon

small bunch of dill, roughly
chopped

salt and pepper

- Cook the cauliflower in a large saucepan of boiling water for 4–5 minutes, until tender. Drain and reserve.

- Meanwhile, melt the butter in a large saucepan over a medium heat, add the onion and leek and cook for 3–4 minutes.

- Add the potatoes and swede to the pan and cook for a further 2 minutes. Pour in the stock and bring to the boil. Cover and simmer for 10 minutes.

- Add the tomatoes and cauliflower and cook for a further 4–5 minutes.

- Gently add the salmon to the soup and cook for 5 minutes, until the fish is just cooked.

- Add the cream, horseradish and lemon juice and stir gently. Sprinkle in the dill and season to taste with salt and pepper.

Smoked Salmon Salad

Divide 250 g (8 oz) mixed salad leaves between 4 plates. Top with 4 sliced ready-cooked fresh beetroot, ¼ sliced cucumber, 8 halved radishes and 12 chopped baby tomatoes, then add 375 g (12 oz) strips of smoked salmon. Whisk 1 teaspoon creamed horseradish into 2 tablespoons of your favourite salad dressing and drizzle over the salad. Sprinkle with 1 tablespoon toasted sesame seeds to serve.

Grilled Salmon with Pan-Fried

Dill Potatoes Cook 500 g (1 lb) peeled and thickly sliced potatoes in a saucepan of boiling water for 10–12 minutes, then drain. Return to the pan and shake the pan to fluff up the edges of the potatoes. Heat 2 tablespoons olive oil in a frying pan, add the potatoes and cook for 8 minutes, turning regularly. Meanwhile, grill 4 x 150 g (5 oz) salmon fillets under a preheated hot grill for 3–4 minutes on each side, or until cooked to your liking. Mix 2 tablespoons creamed horseradish with 5 tablespoons natural yogurt, then stir in ¼ grated cucumber. Toss the potatoes with 2 tablespoons chopped dill and season well with salt and pepper. Serve the salmon on a bed of dill potatoes, with a dollop of the horseradish yogurt.

 **Leek and Rocket Soup**

Serves 4

1 tablespoon olive oil, plus extra
  to serve
500 g (1 lb) leeks, sliced
500 ml (17 fl oz) vegetable stock
60 g (2½ oz) rocket leaves
125 ml (4 fl oz) crème fraîche
200 ml (7 fl oz) soya milk
salt and pepper

- Heat the oil in a saucepan over a medium heat, add the leeks and cook for 8–10 minutes until softening.

- Pour in the stock, add the rocket leaves and simmer for 4–6 minutes.

- Add the crème fraîche and milk, then blend until smooth, using a hand-held blender. Bring back to a simmer and season with salt and pepper. Drizzle over a little olive oil to serve.

 Leek, Rocket and Chicken Soup
Heat a 600 g (1¼ lb) carton of ready-made leek and potato soup in a saucepan according to the pack instructions. Meanwhile, shred 2 cooked chicken breasts. Stir the chicken and 25 g (1 oz) rocket leaves into the hot soup and top with a dollop of natural yogurt to serve.

 Individual Leek Frittatas with Rocket Salad Brush the holes of 2 x 12 bun tins with a little olive oil. Heat 1 tablespoon olive oil in a frying pan and cook 1 large leek, diced, for 4–5 minutes. Meanwhile, mix together 6 eggs, 185 ml (6½ fl oz) double cream, 40 g (1¾ oz) grated Gruyère and 30 g (1¼ oz) grated Parmesan. Stir in the leeks and season with salt and pepper, then pour into the prepared bun tins. Bake in a preheated oven, 200°C (400°F), Gas Mark 6, for 20 minutes, or until just set. Meanwhile, toss together 40 g (1¾ oz) rocket leaves, 12 quartered baby tomatoes, 2 peeled and grated carrots and 1 finely sliced red onion. Toss the salad with your favourite ready-made dressing and serve with the frittatas.

GLU-SOUP-FOL

20 Spicy Sweet Potato and Red Pepper Soup

Serves 4

2 tablespoons vegetable oil

1 red onion, chopped

1 red pepper, deseeded and chopped

550 g (1 lb 2 oz) sweet potatoes, peeled and chopped

¼ teaspoon ground cumin

8 baby tomatoes

1.2 litres (2 pints) vegetable stock

25 g (1 oz) creamed coconut, chopped

salt and pepper

To serve

natural yogurt

coriander sprigs

- Heat the oil in a saucepan over a medium heat, add the onion and pepper and cook for 3–4 minutes. Stir in the sweet potatoes, cumin and tomatoes, and cook for a further 2–3 minutes.

- Pour in the stock, bring to the boil and simmer for 12 minutes. Stir in the creamed coconut and cook for a further 2–3 minutes. Using a hand-held blender, blend the soup until smooth.

- Season with salt and pepper and serve topped with a dollop of natural yogurt and a sprig of coriander.

---

1 Sweet Potato Salad Heat 1 tablespoon olive oil in a frying pan and cook 500 g (1 lb) sweet potatoes, peeled and diced, with 2 deseeded and chopped red peppers for 8–9 minutes, stirring from time to time, until softened. Meanwhile, toss together 150 g (5 oz) baby spinach leaves with 40 g (1¾ oz) watercress, 2 chopped spring onions, 16 halved baby tomatoes and 2–3 tablespoons ready-made salad dressing. To serve, toss in the sweet potato and pepper and sprinkle with 3 tablespoons toasted pumpkin seeds.

3 Warm Sweet Potato Wedges Salad Slice 900 g (1¾ lb) sweet potatoes into wedges. In a large bowl, mix together 2 crushed garlic cloves, 4 tablespoons olive oil, 2 teaspoons chopped sage, 1 teaspoon paprika and some salt and pepper. Toss the potato in the herb and spice mixture, place in a roasting tin and roast in a preheated oven, 200°C (400°F), Gas Mark 6, for 25 minutes. Serve the potato wedges tossed with 250 g (8 oz) baby spinach leaves and 4 chopped spring onions.

30 Smoked Haddock and Potato Chowder

Serves 4

1 tablespoon olive oil

1 onion, chopped

2 celery sticks, sliced

375 g (12 oz) new potatoes, cut into bite-sized pieces

600 ml (1 pint) vegetable stock

600 ml (1 pint) milk

375 g (12 oz) smoked haddock, cut into bite-sized pieces

1 tablespoon freshly chopped parsley, to serve

- Heat the oil in a large saucepan over a medium heat, add the onion and celery and cook for 4–5 minutes, until soft.
- Add the potatoes and stir-fry for 2 minutes.
- Pour in the stock and bring to the boil, then simmer for 13–15 minutes, until the potatoes are tender.
- Pour in the milk and bring back to the boil. Add the fish and cook for 4–5 minutes.
- Serve sprinkled with the parsley.

 Smoked Haddock and Potato Salad

Place 4 x 150 g (5 oz) smoked haddock fillets in a large shallow pan and cover with 300 ml (½ pint) milk. Bring to the boil, then lower the heat and simmer for 8–9 minutes, until the fish is cooked. Meanwhile, poach 4 eggs in a frying pan of simmering water for 4–5 minutes. Stir 2 teaspoons creamed horseradish into 200 g (7 oz) ready-made potato salad and divide between 4 plates. Top each with a piece of fish and a poached egg. Sprinkle with 2 tablespoons chopped chives to serve.

 New Potato and Smoked Haddock Salad Cook 500 g (1 lb) halved new potatoes in a pan of boiling water for 10–12 minutes, until tender, then drain. Heat 2 tablespoons olive oil in a frying pan, add the potatoes and cook for 5–6 minutes, turning frequently, until lightly golden. Meanwhile, poach 600 g (1¼ lb) smoked haddock fillets in 300 ml (½ pint) milk for 8–9 minutes, drain and break into large flakes. Whisk together 1 tablespoon wholegrain mustard, 5 tablespoons extra virgin olive oil, 1 teaspoon clear honey and 1 tablespoon white wine vinegar. Toss 125 g (4 oz) salad leaves, 4 sliced spring onions and 12 halved baby tomatoes in the dressing, then add the potatoes and fish and combine very gently to serve.

Pea and Ham Soup

Serves 4

1 tablespoon olive oil
2 shallots, diced
400 g (13 oz) frozen peas
350 ml (12 fl oz) vegetable or
  chicken stock
150 ml (¼ pint) double cream
125 g (4 oz) shredded ham

To serve

2 tablespoons crème fraîche
small handful of watercress

- Heat the oil in a large saucepan, add the shallots and cook for 2 minutes. Add the peas and stock and bring to the boil, then lower the heat and simmer for 2–3 minutes.

- Remove from the heat and pour in the cream. Using a hand-held blender, blend the soup until smooth. Season to taste with salt and pepper.

- Gently reheat the soup and stir in the shredded ham. Serve topped with a dollop of crème fraîche and some watercress.

Pea and Ham Frittata Salad

Heat 1 tablespoon olive oil in an ovenproof frying pan over a medium heat, add 4 chopped rashers of unsmoked streaky bacon and 2 diced shallots and cook for 1–2 minutes. Remove with a slotted spoon and reserve. Whisk together 6 large eggs, then add the bacon, 100 g (3½ oz) thawed frozen peas, 125 g (4 oz) chopped ham and 1 tablespoon chopped parsley. Pour the egg mixture into the frying pan and cook for 12–15 minutes over a medium heat until the underneath is cooked. Sprinkle over 75 g (3 oz) grated Cheddar, then place the frittata under a preheated hot grill for 2–3 minutes until the top is golden and bubbling. Meanwhile, toss 250 g (8 oz) salad leaves with your favourite dressing. To turn the frittata out of the frying pan, place a plate on top and turn upside down. Cut into wedges and serve on a bed of salad.

Pea and Ham Rice Stir-Fry

Cook 150 g (5 oz) basmati rice for 8–10 minutes, or according to the pack instructions. Lightly beat 3 eggs with 1 teaspoon each oyster sauce and soy sauce. Heat 1 tablespoon oil in a wok, add the eggs and scramble lightly, then remove and reserve. Add another tablespoon of oil and stir-fry 4 chopped spring onions for 1 minute, then add 275 g (9 oz) chopped ham and 175 g (6 oz) thawed frozen peas. Cook for 2–3 minutes then remove from the pan. Add the rice to the pan, stir in 2–3 teaspoons each tamari soy sauce and oyster sauce and cook for 2–3 minutes. Return the ham and pea mixture to the pan with the scrambled egg and stir-fry for 3–4 minutes.

Butter Bean, Tomato and Feta Salad

Serves 4

400 g (13 oz) can butter beans, rinsed and drained
18 cherry tomatoes, halved
½ cucumber, chopped
175 g (6 oz) feta cheese, crumbled
juice of 1 lemon
1 teaspoon dried chilli flakes
2 tablespoons olive oil
60 g (2½ oz) watercress
2 teaspoons sunflower seeds
1 teaspoon pumpkin seeds
½ teaspoon sesame seeds

- Place the butter beans, cherry tomatoes, cucumber and feta in a large bowl.

- In another bowl, whisk together the lemon juice, chilli flakes and oil to make a dressing.

- Divide the watercress between 4 plates or shallow bowls.

- Toast the sunflower, pumpkin and sesame seeds together in a small pan over a low heat until starting to turn golden.

- Pour the dressing over the butter bean mixture and combine well.

- Spoon the butter bean mixture over the watercress, then sprinkle with the toasted seeds to serve.

 Butter Bean Soup with Crumbled Feta Heat 1 tablespoon olive oil in a large saucepan, add 1 chopped onion and 2 sliced celery sticks and cook for 2–3 minutes. Stir in 2 teaspoons ground cumin and cook for a further 2 minutes. Pour in 600 ml (1 pint) vegetable stock, a 400 g (13 oz) can butter beans, rinsed and drained, and a 400 g (13 oz) can chopped tomatoes. Season with salt and pepper and simmer for 8 minutes. Add 100 g (3½ oz) broad beans, 1 tablespoon chopped coriander leaves and the juice of ½ lemon and cook for a further 2–3 minutes. Sprinkle with 125 g (4 oz) crumbled feta.

 Butter Bean and Tomato Curry Heat 1 tablespoon olive oil in a pan over a medium heat, then add 1 chopped onion, 2 deseeded and chopped red peppers and 2 crushed garlic cloves and cook for 5–6 minutes. Stir in 1 teaspoon ground cumin and ½ teaspoon each of ground coriander, turmeric and chilli powder. Cook for 1–2 minutes. Stir in 4 chopped tomatoes and 2 x 400 g (13 oz) cans of butter beans, rinsed and drained. Mash a few of the butter beans, then cover the pan and simmer for 8–10 minutes. Stir in a peeled and grated 5 cm (2 inch) piece of fresh root ginger and a pinch of garam masala and cook for a further 2–3 minutes. Stir in 2 tablespoons chopped coriander. Serve with steamed basmati rice.

Roasted Potato and Tomato Salad with Honeyed Goats' Cheese

Serves 4

450 g (14½ oz) new potatoes, halved

2 tablespoons olive oil

4 vines of baby tomatoes (about 125 g/4 oz each)

4 slices of goats' cheese (100 g/3½ oz each)

2 teaspoons clear honey

1 tablespoon balsamic vinegar

100 g (3½ oz) baby spinach leaves

50 g (2 oz) chopped walnuts

salt and pepper

- Blanch the potatoes in large saucepan of boiling water for 3–4 minutes, then drain.

- Pour the oil into a roasting pan and place in a preheated oven, 200°C (400°F), Gas Mark 6, for 1–2 minutes. Add the potatoes to the hot pan, season well with salt and pepper and roast for 15 minutes.

- Add the tomatoes to the pan and roast for a further 5 minutes.

- Meanwhile, place the goats' cheese on a baking sheet, and pour ½ teaspoon honey over each slice. Cook under a preheated hot grill for 6–8 minutes, until golden and bubbling.

- Divide the spinach leaves between 4 shallow bowls and spoon over the potatoes and tomatoes. Pour the vinegar into the roasting pan and mix with the pan juices.

- Place the goats' cheese on the salad, sprinkle over the chopped walnuts and drizzle with the pan juices.

 Grilled Goats' Cheese with Vine Tomato Salsa Place 4 x 100 g (3½ oz) slices of goats' cheese on a baking sheet and pour ½ teaspoon honey over each one. Cook under a preheated hot grill for 6–8 minutes, until golden and bubbling. Meanwhile, dice 200 g (7 oz) vine tomatoes, 1 small red onion and 1 peeled and stoned avocado and mix together with 2 teaspoons red wine vinegar. Serve the goats' cheese on baby spinach leaves with the salsa spooned over.

 Roasted Vine Tomato Soup with Goats' Cheese Place 6 large tomatoes, still on the vine, in a roasting tin with 1 large chopped onion, 1 garlic bulb, halved horizontally, 5 black peppercorns, 2–3 thyme sprigs and 2 tablespoons olive oil. Roast in a preheated oven, 200°C (400°F), Gas Mark 6, for 15 minutes. Remove the tomato stalks, thyme stalks and black peppercorns, then squeeze out the garlic bulbs and place them in a blender or food processor

with the remaining contents of the roasting tin, 200 g (7 oz) sun-dried tomatoes and 600 ml (1 pint) vegetable stock. Blend until smooth. Pour the soup into a pan to reheat and serve sprinkled with 100 g (3½ oz) crumbled goats' cheese and a few thyme leaves.

Quick Watercress, Beetroot and Orange Salad

Serves 4

75 g (3 oz) watercress

25 g (1 oz) rocket leaves

1 orange, segmented

4 ready-cooked fresh beetroot, cut into wedges

½ cucumber, chopped

2 tablespoons walnuts

100 g (3½ oz) feta cheese

ready-made salad dressing of choice, to serve

- In a large bowl, toss together the watercress, rocket, orange segments, beetroot, cucumber and walnuts.

- Crumble over the feta cheese and drizzle with the salad dressing to serve.

2 Watercress and Orange Soup

Heat 1 tablespoon olive oil in a saucepan over a medium heat, add 1 chopped onion and cook for 2–3 minutes, until starting to soften. Add 1 large diced potato and 150 g (5 oz) watercress and cook for 1–2 minutes, then pour in the juice of 1 orange and 1 litre (1¾ pints) vegetable stock. Simmer for 10–12 minutes, until the potato is cooked. Stir in the grated rind of 1 orange, then, using a hand-held blender, blend the soup until smooth. Season to taste with salt and pepper and serve with a swirl of cream.

3 Spiced Watercress, Beetroot and Orange Salad

Place 2 raw beetroot, peeled and cut into chunks, in a roasting tin and sprinkle with ½ tablespoon olive oil and ½ teaspoon cumin seeds. Roast in a preheated oven, 200°C (400°F), Gas Mark 6, for 15–20 minutes, until tender. Toss together 80 g (3 oz) watercress, 2 segmented oranges and 1 large carrot, peeled and grated. Divide the salad between 4 plates, then top with the beetroot and 100 g (3½ oz) sliced or crumbled goats' cheese. Sprinkle over 25 g (1 oz) roughly broken pecan nuts. Whisk together 2 tablespoons extra virgin olive oil, 1 tablespoon lemon juice, 1 teaspoon clear honey, ½ teaspoon Dijon mustard, ½ teaspoon freshly chopped rosemary and some pepper, then pour the dressing over the salad.

30 Roasted Cauliflower and Cashew Nut Salad

Serves 4

1 large cauliflower, cut into florets
400 g (13 oz) can chickpeas, rinsed and drained
1 teaspoon cumin seeds
1 teaspoon coriander seeds
½ teaspoon ground turmeric
½ teaspoon ground ginger
½ teaspoon garam masala
4 tablespoons olive oil
100 g (3½ oz) cashew nuts
150 g (5 oz) natural yogurt
4 tablespoons lemon juice
½ teaspoon Dijon mustard
150 g (5 oz) baby spinach leaves
salt and pepper

- Place the cauliflower in a roasting tin with the chickpeas, spices, some salt and pepper and 2 tablespoons of the oil. Roast in a preheated oven, 220°C (425°F) Gas Mark 7, for 15 minutes, then toss in the cashew nuts and roast for a further 10 minutes.

- Meanwhile, whisk together the remaining oil, yogurt, lemon juice and mustard to make a dressing.

- Put the spinach on a large serving plate and spoon over the spiced cauliflower.

- Drizzle with the yogurt dressing and serve.

1 Raw Cauliflower and Cashew Nut Salad Chop 1 large cauliflower into small florets, then place in a food processor and pulse once to break them down. Whisk together 1 teaspoon grated fresh root ginger, 1½ tablespoons sesame oil, ½ tablespoon soy sauce, 1 tablespoon white wine vinegar and ½ crushed garlic clove. Mix 50 g (2 oz) roughly chopped cashew nuts, a bunch of roughly chopped coriander leaves and ½ tablespoon sesame seeds into the cauliflower, toss with the dressing and spoon over a large plate of salad leaves.

2 Cauliflower and Cashew Nut Soup Heat 1 tablespoon olive oil in a large saucepan over a medium heat, add 1 chopped onion and 1 chopped leek and cook for 2–3 minutes. Add ½ teaspoon curry powder, 1 large cauliflower, cut into florets, and 1 peeled and grated parsnip. Pour in 1.2 litres (2 pints) vegetable stock, bring to the boil and then simmer for 10 minutes. Process 50 g (2 oz) cashew nuts in a blender, then add 200 ml (7 fl oz) of the soup and blend again until smooth. Add this to the soup to thicken it, then bring it back to a simmer.

Season with salt and pepper and serve with a drizzle of single cream on top.

30 Chickpea, Tomato and Pepper Salad

Serves 4

3 large red peppers, deseeded and cut into quarters

6 plum tomatoes, halved

4 tablespoons olive oil

1 teaspoon cumin seeds

1 tablespoon lemon juice

½ teaspoon Dijon mustard

½ teaspoon clear honey

400 g (13 oz) can chickpeas, drained

10–12 basil leaves, roughly torn

100 g (3½ oz) baby spinach leaves

salt and pepper

- Place the peppers and tomatoes in a roasting tin and toss with 1 tablespoon of the oil and the cumin seeds. Season with salt and pepper and roast in a preheated oven, 220°C (425°F), Gas Mark 7, for 20 minutes.

- Whisk the remaining oil with the lemon juice, mustard and honey to make a dressing.

- Remove the peppers from the oven and spoon into a bowl. Stir in the chickpeas, basil and spinach, pour over the dressing and serve immediately.

10 Chickpea, Tomato and Pepper Soup

Heat 1 tablespoon olive oil in a large saucepan over a medium heat, add 1 deseeded and chopped red pepper and 1 diced red onion and cook for 1–2 minutes. Stir in a 400 g (13 oz) can of chickpeas, rinsed and drained, and 3 chopped plum tomatoes. Pour in 900 ml (1½ pints) vegetable stock and season well. Simmer for 4–5 minutes. Using a hand-held blender, blend until smooth and serve with a drizzle of olive oil.

20 Chillied Chickpea, Red Pepper and Feta Salad

Halve and deseed 3 red peppers and place on a baking sheet. Cook under a preheated hot grill for 8–10 minutes until blackened. Place in a bowl, cover with clingfilm and leave until cool enough to handle. Heat 1 tablespoon olive oil in a saucepan over a medium heat, add 1 deseeded and sliced red chilli, 2 sliced garlic cloves and 4 spring onions and cook for 2–3 minutes. Remove from the heat and stir in a 400 g (13 oz) can of chickpeas, rinsed and drained, 100 g (3½ oz) halved baby tomatoes and 100 g (3½ oz) baby spinach leaves. Whisk together 2 tablespoons extra virgin olive oil, 2 tablespoons lemon juice and a pinch of paprika. Peel the blackened skin off the peppers and cut into slices. Mix the peppers into the chickpea salad with the dressing and serve sprinkled with 125 g (4 oz) crumbled feta.

 # Butternut Squash, Asparagus and Parma Ham Salad

Serves 4

1 kg (2 lb) butternut squash, peeled, deseeded and cut into chunks

2 red onions, cut into wedges

2 tablespoons pumpkin seeds

1 tablespoon olive oil

175 g (6 oz) asparagus tips

12 slices of Parma ham

2 tablespoons extra virgin olive oil

1 tablespoon balsamic vinegar

2 chicory bulbs, leaves separated

salt and pepper

- Place the butternut squash and onions in a roasting tin, sprinkle in the pumpkin seeds and toss with the olive oil and some salt and pepper.

- Roast in a preheated oven, 200°C (400°F), Gas Mark 6, for 22 minutes, until starting to caramelize, then toss in the asparagus tips and roast for a further 5 minutes.

- Place the Parma ham under a preheated hot grill for 4–5 minutes until crisp.

- Whisk the extra virgin olive oil with the vinegar to make a dressing.

- Divide the chicory leaves between 4 plates and top with the roasted vegetables and Parma ham.

- Drizzle with the dressing and serve.

 Asparagus-Parma Wraps with Butternut Squash Soup Wrap 12 spears of asparagus in 12 slices of Parma ham and place on a baking sheet. Drizzle with 1 tablespoon olive oil and bake in a preheated oven, 200°C (400°F), Gas Mark 6, for 3–4 minutes. Meanwhile, heat 2 x 600 g (1¼ lb) cartons of ready-made butternut squash soup according to the pack instructions. Serve the soup with the asparagus wraps on the side.

 Butternut Squash Soup with Parma Ham Heat 1 tablespoon olive oil in a saucepan over a medium heat, add 2 chopped onions, 1 crushed garlic clove and 1 deseeded and diced red chilli and cook for 2–3 minutes. Add 1 kg (2 lb) peeled and chopped butternut squash and cook for a further 2–3 minutes, then pour in 900 ml (1½ pints) vegetable stock, bring to the boil and simmer for 15 minutes, until the squash is tender. Meanwhile, grill 6 slices of Parma ham until crisp, then roughly break up. Using a hand-held blender, blend the soup until smooth. Serve with a swirl of crème fraîche and a sprinkling of Parma ham pieces.

10 Salmon and Watercress Salad

Serves 4

3 tablespoons extra virgin olive oil
juice of 1 orange
½ teaspoon mustard
½ teaspoon caster sugar
75 g (3 oz) watercress
¼ cucumber, chopped
2 oranges, peeled and segmented
2 tablespoons toasted walnuts
1 avocado, peeled, stoned and
  sliced
175 g (6 oz) smoked salmon strips
4 gluten-free pitta breads,
  toasted, to serve (optional)

- Whisk together the oil, orange juice, mustard and sugar in a small bowl to make a dressing.

- In a large bowl, toss together the watercress, cucumber, oranges, walnuts and avocado.

- Toss with the dressing and smoked salmon and serve with the toasted pitta breads, if liked.

20 Grilled Salmon with Potato and Watercress Salad

Cook 500 g (1 lb) new potatoes, halved if large, in a saucepan of boiling water for 15–16 minutes, until tender. Meanwhile, in a large bowl mix together 2 diced shallots, 1 tablespoon roughly chopped capers, 3 tablespoons mayonnaise, 1 tablespoon creamed horseradish and 1 tablespoon chopped chives. Under a preheated hot grill, cook 4 x 150 g (5 oz) salmon fillets for 4–5 minutes on each side, or until cooked to your liking. Toast 2 tablespoons pumpkin seeds for 1–2 minutes in a dry frying pan. Drain the potatoes and toss in the mayonnaise mixture with 30 g (1¼ oz) roughly torn watercress. Serve the salmon with the potato and watercress salad, sprinkled with toasted pumpkin seeds.

30 Salmon, Watercress and Potato Soup

Heat 1 tablespoon olive oil in a large saucepan over a medium heat, add 1 chopped onion and cook for 3–4 minutes, then stir in 350 g (11½ oz) peeled and chopped potatoes. Pour in 1.2 litres (2 pints) vegetable stock and simmer for 18–20 minutes. Stir in 225 g (7½ oz) watercress and cook for 1–2 minutes until it has wilted. Blend the soup, using a hand-held blender, until smooth. Stir in 2 tablespoons crème fraîche and season. Bring back to a simmer, add 175 g (6 oz) salmon fillet cut into chunks and cook for 2–3 minutes, then serve.

GLU-SOUP-SIV

Sesame Seared Tuna with Spicy Coriander Salad

Serves 4

2 x 150 g (5 oz) tuna steaks

4 tablespoons tamari soy sauce

2 teaspoons clear honey

4 cm (1¾ inch) piece of fresh root ginger, peeled and grated

½ cucumber, cut into matchsticks

3 carrots, peeled and cut into matchsticks

6 spring onions, shredded

small handful of coriander leaves

2–3 tablespoons sesame seeds

1½ tablespoons lime juice

- Place the tuna in a non-metallic bowl with the soy sauce, honey and ginger and leave to stand for 15 minutes, turning once.

- Meanwhile, mix together the cucumber, carrots, spring onions and coriander.

- Roll the tuna in the sesame seeds. Heat a griddle pan until hot then cook the tuna steaks for 2–3 minutes on each side (the inside should still be pink). Leave to rest for 2 minutes, then slice thinly and serve on the cucumber salad, sprinkled with lime juice.

Coriander-Spiced Tuna with Salad Place 20 g (¾ oz) coriander leaves, 3 garlic cloves, 2 cm (¾ inch) piece of peeled and chopped fresh root ginger and 1 tablespoon lemon juice in a small blender and blend. Gradually add 150 ml (¼ pint) olive oil to make a thick smooth sauce. Pour the sauce over 4 x 150 g (5 oz) tuna steaks. Heat a griddle pan until hot and cook the tuna steaks for 2–4 minutes, turning once (cook for longer if you do not like your tuna pink). Serve with a crisp green salad.

Seared Tuna with Coriander-Roasted Tomato Salad In a small bowl, mix together 3 tablespoons olive oil, 3 tablespoons balsamic vinegar and 1 tablespoon crushed coriander seeds. Place 400 g (13 oz) baby vine tomatoes in a roasting tray and pour over the vinegar mixture. Roast in a preheated oven, 200°C (400°F) Gas Mark 6 for 15 minutes. Meanwhile, heat a griddle pan and cook 4 x 150 g (5 oz) tuna steaks for 2 minutes on each side (longer if you do not like your tuna pink). Serve the tuna with the balsamic tomatoes on a bed of rocket leaves, scattered with 2 tablespoons roughly chopped coriander leaves

Beef Carpaccio and Bean Salad

Serves 4

250 g (8 oz) beef fillet
3 tablespoons extra virgin olive oil
1 teaspoon black pepper
1 tablespoon chopped thyme leaves
1 teaspoon Dijon mustard
½ tablespoon balsamic vinegar
½ teaspoon clear honey
125 g (4 oz) green beans, trimmed
400 g (13 oz) can cannellini beans, rinsed and drained
25g (1 oz) Parmesan cheese shavings, to garnish

- Place the beef fillet on a chopping board and rub with 1 tablespoon of the oil, the pepper and the thyme. Wrap in clingfilm and place in the freezer for 20 minutes.

- Meanwhile, whisk together the remaining oil with the mustard, vinegar and honey to make a dressing.

- Blanch the green beans for 2–3 minutes in boiling water, then refresh under cold running water. Toss the green beans and cannellini beans in the dressing and leave to stand at room temperature.

- Unwrap the beef fillet, slice as thinly as possible and arrange on a platter. Spoon over the bean salad, with all the dressing, and garnish with shavings of Parmesan.

---

1 **Quick Beef Carpaccio and Bean Salad** Whisk together 3 tablespoons olive oil, 1 tablespoon balsamic vinegar, 1 teaspoon mustard and 1 teaspoon honey. Blanch 125 g (4 oz) green beans for 2–3 minutes in boiling water, then refresh under cold running water. Toss in the dressing with a 400 g (13 oz) can cannellini beans, rinsed and drained, and leave to stand at room temperature. Arrange 200 g (7 oz) thinly sliced shop-bought beef carpaccio on a platter, spoon over the bean salad and garnish with shavings of Parmesan.

2 **Nutty Beef and Bean Salad** Rub 450 g (14½ oz) rump steak with 1 tablespoon olive oil and sprinkle with 1 tablespoon black pepper. Fry the steak for 1–2 minutes on each side in 1 tablespoon olive oil, then leave to rest. In a large bowl, toss together 40 g (1¾ oz) lamb's lettuce, 2 chopped ready-cooked beetroots, 4 sliced spring onions, a 400 g (13 oz) can butter beans, rinsed and drained, 12 halved baby plum tomatoes and 2 tablespoons toasted cashew nuts. Whisk together 3 tablespoons extra virgin olive oil, 1 tablespoon balsamic vinegar, 1 crushed garlic clove, 1 teaspoon soft dark brown sugar and ½ teaspoon wholegrain mustard, then stir in 1 tablespoon roughly chopped peanuts. Slice the steak and place on top of the salad, then pour over the dressing to serve.

 # Honey and Mustard Chicken Salad

Serves 4

3 tablespoons extra virgin olive oil

1 teaspoon clear honey

1 teaspoon Dijon mustard

1 teaspoon lemon juice

3 skinless chicken breasts

2 tablespoons pumpkin seeds

75 g (3 oz) watercress

25 g (1 oz) rocket

200 g (7 oz) frozen peas, thawed

1 large avocado, peeled, stoned and cut into slices

- In a small bowl, whisk together the olive oil, honey, mustard and lemon juice to make a dressing.

- Place the chicken breasts on a foil-lined baking sheet. Cook under a preheated hot grill for 5–6 minutes on each side, until cooked through.

- Meanwhile, heat a small frying pan over a medium heat, add the pumpkin seeds and dry-roast until golden, stirring frequently.

- Toss together the watercress and rocket and divide between 4 plates.

- Slice the chicken diagonally and divide between the plates of salad leaves. Scatter over the peas, avocado and pumpkin seeds, pour over the dressing and serve immediately.

---

1 **Chicken, Avocado, Watercress and Mustard Sandwich** Spread 4 slices of gluten-free bread with 1 teaspoon wholegrain mustard. Divide 25 g (1 oz) watercress between the slices of bread, then top with 2 sliced honey-roasted chicken breasts and 1 large peeled, stoned and sliced avocado. Top with 4 more slices of gluten-free bread to make 4 sandwiches.

3 **Chicken Kebab Salad with Honey-Mustard Dressing** In a large bowl, mix together 4 tablespoons clear honey, 3 tablespoons each sunflower oil and tamari soy sauce and 2 crushed garlic cloves. Stir in 4 skinless chicken breasts cut into bite-sized pieces and 2 deseeded red peppers, cut into chunks. Leave to marinate for 10 minutes. Thread the chicken and pepper onto 8 skewers, presoaked in water to prevent burning, and cook under a preheated hot grill for 12–15 minutes, until the chicken is cooked through, turning once. Meanwhile, toss together 75 g (3 oz) watercress and 25 g (1 oz) rocket with 1 peeled, stoned and sliced avocado. Whisk together 3 tablespoons olive oil and 1 tablespoon white wine vinegar, 1 teaspoon clear honey and 1 teaspoon Dijon mustard and drizzle over the salad. Serve the kebabs on a bed of salad.

Peppered Steak and Red Onion Salad

Serves 4

2 red onions, cut into wedges
5 tablespoons olive oil
1 teaspoon thyme leaves
1½ tablespoons balsamic vinegar
1 teaspoon wholegrain mustard
1 teaspoon clear honey
4 x 150–175 g (5–6 oz) sirloin steaks, at room temperature
2–3 tablespoons pepper
250 g (8 oz) mixed salad leaves

- Place the onions in a roasting tin, sprinkle over 1 tablespoon of the oil and the thyme and toss together. Roast in a preheated oven, 220°C (425°F), Gas Mark 7, for 15–18 minutes.

- Meanwhile, whisk together 3 tablespoons of the remaining oil with 1 tablespoon of the vinegar, the mustard and honey to make a dressing.

- Dust the steaks with the pepper on both sides.

- Heat a griddle until really hot and add the remaining olive oil. Cook the steaks for 2–3 minutes on each side, depending on how pink you like your steak. Leave to rest for 2–3 minutes.

- Remove the onions from the oven and sprinkle over the remaining vinegar.

- Toss the salad leaves with the dressing and add the balsamic onions. Serve with the steaks.

 Steak and Red Onion Sandwich
Slice 4 gluten-free baguettes in half horizontally and toast each side. Cook 400 g (13 oz) sirloin steak on a hot griddle for 2–3 minutes each side, or until cooked to your liking. Spread the bottom half of each baguette with 2 teaspoons wholegrain mustard and top with 30 g (1 ¼ oz) rocket leaves. Slice the steak and place on the rocket along with a thinly sliced small red onion. Top with the remaining baguette halves to make 4 sandwiches.

 Steak with Red Onion Marmalade and Rocket Mash Heat 1 tablespoon olive oil in a saucepan over a medium heat, add 3 sliced red onions and cook for 1–2 minutes. Stir in 2 tablespoons balsamic vinegar, 3 tablespoons dark brown sugar and a drizzle of honey, then reduce the heat, cover with a piece of greaseproof paper and cook for 25 minutes, stirring from time to time. Meanwhile, cook 875 g (1¾ lb) peeled potatoes in a saucepan of boiling water until tender. Heat a griddle pan until hot, drizzle in a little olive oil and cook 4 x 150 g (5 oz) steaks for 2–3 minutes on each side, or until cooked to your liking. Leave to rest. Drain and mash the potatoes with 50 g (2 oz) butter and a handful of rocket leaves. Serve the steak with the rocket mash and red onion marmalade.

Quinoa and Feta Salad with Roast Vegetables

Serves 4

1 red pepper, deseeded and cut into chunks

1 yellow pepper, deseeded and cut into chunks

1 red onion, cut into wedges

2 courgettes, sliced

2 garlic cloves

100 g (3½ oz) butternut squash, peeled and cut into chunks

2 tablespoons olive oil

200 g (7 oz) quinoa

200 g (7 oz) feta cheese, crumbled

small handful of parsley, roughly chopped

salt and pepper

- Place the peppers, onion, courgettes, garlic and squash in a roasting tin and toss with the oil. Roast in a preheated oven, 200°C (400°F), Gas Mark 6, for 26–28 minutes.

- Meanwhile, cook the quinoa in boiling water for 8–9 minutes, or according to the pack instructions. Drain and refresh under cold running water, then set aside.

- Remove the vegetables from the oven. Remove the garlic cloves, squeeze out the flesh and return it to the vegetables. Season well with salt and pepper.

- Stir the quinoa, feta and parsley into the vegetables and serve.

Quinoa, Feta and Raw Vegetable Salad Cook 50 g (2 oz) quinoa in boiling water for 8–9 minutes or according to the pack instructions. Meanwhile, in a large bowl, mix together 2 diced large tomatoes, ½ diced cucumber, small bunch each of parsley and mint, chopped, 1 diced small red onion, 50 g (2 oz) shredded mangetout and 1 deseeded and diced red pepper. Drain and refresh the quinoa under cold running water, then stir into the salad ingredients with 2–3 tablespoons of ready-made vinaigrette and 100 g (3½ oz) crumbled feta.

Quinoa and Vegetable Soup with Feta Cook 75 g (3 oz) quinoa in boiling water for 8–9 minutes, or according to the pack instructions. Drain and refresh under cold running water. Meanwhile, heat 2 tablespoons olive oil in a saucepan over a medium heat, add 1 diced onion and cook for 2–3 minutes. Add 2 crushed garlic cloves and cook for a further 2 minutes. Add 2 peeled and chopped carrots, 2 sliced celery sticks, 1 chopped courgette, 100 g (3½ oz) peas and 1 deseeded and chopped red pepper and cook for a further 2–3 minutes. Pour in 1.2 litres (2 pints) vegetable stock and simmer for 15 minutes. Stir in the cooked quinoa and 2 tablespoons chopped parsley. Serve in warmed bowls with 100 g (3½ oz) crumbled feta sprinkled over the top.

QuickCook
Family
Suppers

Recipes listed by cooking time

30

20

10

10 Homemade Fish Fingers

Serves 4

3 tablespoons plain gluten-free flour
1 large egg, beaten
30 g (1¼ oz) gluten-free breadcrumbs
25 g (1 oz) polenta
500 g (1 lb) cod fillet, cut into 8 thick pieces
3 tablespoons sunflower oil
200 g (7 oz) frozen peas
2 tablespoons butter or olive oil
4 eggs

- Place the flour and the beaten egg in two separate shallow bowls, then mix the breadcrumbs and polenta together in a third bowl.

- Gently toss the pieces of fish first in the flour, then in the egg and finally in the breadcrumb and polenta mixture to coat.

- Heat the sunflower oil in a frying pan over a medium heat and cook the fish fingers carefully for 5–6 minutes, turning occasionally, until golden.

- Meanwhile, cook the peas in boiling water for 2–3 minutes.

- Heat the butter or olive oil in another frying pan and fry the eggs to your liking.

- Drain the peas and serve with the fish fingers and fried eggs.

2 Herbed Fish with Asparagus and Peas

Mix together 25 g (1 oz) gluten-free breadcrumbs, 25 g (1 oz) polenta, 25 g (1 oz) grated Parmesan, the grated rind of 1 lemon and 1 tablespoon chopped parsley. Boil 175 g (6 oz) peas for 2–3 minutes. Toss 200 g (7 oz) asparagus in 1 tablespoon olive oil and cook on a hot griddle for 5–6 minutes, tossing regularly. Meanwhile, fry 4 x 150 g (5 oz) cod loin fillets in 1 tablespoon oil for 2–3 minutes, then turn over, sprinkle with the crumb mixture and cook for a further 1–2 minutes. Place under a hot grill for 1–2 minutes, until the crust is golden. Toss the vegetables with 1 tablespoon chopped mint.

3 Roasted Fish with Pea and Mint Mash

Cook 625 g (1¼ lb) potatoes, peeled and cut into chunks, in boiling water for 12–15 minutes, adding 125 g (4 oz) frozen peas 2 minutes before the end of the cooking time. Meanwhile, heat 1 tablespoon olive oil in a saucepan over a medium heat and cook 4 x 150 g (5 oz) cod fillets, skin side down, for 2–3 minutes, until the skin is crisp. Place in a roasting tin, and add 500 g (1 lb) halved baby tomatoes, 50 g (2 oz) halved olives and 25 g (1 oz) pine nuts. Season well with salt and pepper. Roast in a preheated oven, 200°C (400°F), Gas Mark 6, for 12–15 minutes, until the fish is tender. Drain the potatoes and peas and mash with 50 g (2 oz) butter and 1 tablespoon chopped mint. Remove the fish from the roasting tin and keep warm. Place the roasting tin on the hob over a medium heat, stir in 2 tablespoons pesto and 2–3 tablespoons olive oil and heat for 1–2 minutes. Place the fish on a bed of mash, pour over the pesto tomato sauce and sprinkle with a few basil leaves to serve.

20 Roast Pork Chops with Apple and Celery Salad

Serves 4

4 x 175 g (6 oz) pork chops
1 tablespoon olive oil
1 teaspoon fennel seeds
2 tablespoons extra virgin olive oil
2 tablespoons red wine vinegar
2–3 sage leaves, chopped
4 dessert apples, cored and thinly
  sliced into rings
3 celery sticks, thickly sliced
12 green grapes, halved
pepper

- Brush the chops with the olive oil and sprinkle with the fennel seeds and pepper.

- Place on a rack over a roasting tray and bake in a preheated oven, 200°C (400°F), Gas Mark 6, for 20 minutes.

- Meanwhile, whisk the extra virgin olive oil, vinegar and sage together to make a dressing.

- Toss the apples, celery and grapes together with the dressing and serve with the roasted chops.

10 Sticky Pork Steaks with Caramelized Apples Melt 25 g (1 oz) butter in a frying pan over a medium heat, add 4 peeled, cored and sliced dessert apples and cook for 6–8 minutes. Mix together 4 teaspoons tomato ketchup, 2 tablespoons soft dark brown sugar, 1 tablespoon white wine vinegar and 1 teaspoon paprika. Heat 1 tablespoon olive oil in another frying pan and cook 4 x 150 g (5 oz) pork steaks for 3–4 minutes on each side. Pour in the sauce and cook for a further 1–2 minutes. Serve the pork chops with the apple and some steamed green vegetables, if liked.

30 Rosemary Pork Chops with Roast Potatoes and Apples Cook 625 g (1¼ lb) potatoes, peeled and cut into chunks, in a large saucepan of boiling water for 12–15 minutes until tender. Drain, return to the pan and shake to rough up the edges of the potatoes. Meanwhile, heat 2 tablespoons olive oil and 25 g (1 oz) butter in a roasting tin in a preheated oven, 200°C (400°F), Gas Mark 6, for 5–6 minutes. Score the fat of 4 x 175 g (6 oz) pork chops with a sharp knife and sprinkle with salt and pepper. Heat a nonstick frying pan and brown the pork chops for 2–3 minutes on each side, then add to the roasting tin with the potatoes, 2–3 sprigs rosemary and 3 cored and chopped apples. Roast for a further 10–12 minutes, until the pork is cooked through and the potatoes are golden.

 Chicken and Cashew Nut Curry

Serves 4

2 teaspoons cumin seeds
1 tablespoon coriander seeds
½ teaspoon fennel seeds
2 curry leaves
2 tablespoons sunflower oil
4 chicken breasts, chopped
1 onion, chopped
2 garlic cloves, crushed
1.2 cm (½ inch) piece of fresh
  root ginger, peeled and grated
1 red chilli, deseeded and diced
500 ml (17 fl oz) chicken stock
75 g (3 oz) creamed coconut,
  chopped
450 g (14½ oz) baby spinach
  leaves
60 g (2½ oz) cashew nuts,
  toasted
2 tablespoons chopped fresh
  coriander

- Heat a small frying pan over a medium heat, add the spices and curry leaves and dry-fry until they are fragrant. Grind in a pestle and mortar or grinder.

- Heat the oil in a saucepan over a medium heat, add the chicken and brown for 3– 4 minutes. Add the onion, garlic, ginger, chilli and ground spice mix and cook for a further 3–4 minutes

- Pour in the chicken stock and creamed coconut and bring to the boil. Simmer for 10–15 minutes, then stir in the spinach and cashew nuts. Season to taste with salt and pepper.

- Sprinkle with the chopped coriander and serve with basmati rice, if liked.

 Chicken and Cashew Salad

Dry-fry 1 teaspoon cumin seeds, ½ teaspoon fennel seeds and 60 g (2½ oz) cashew nuts for 3 minutes. Toss together 1 roughly torn cos lettuce, 25 g (1 oz) rocket leaves, 1 small sliced red onion and a handful of coriander leaves with the nuts and 3 sliced cooked chicken breasts. Whisk together 3 tablespoons olive oil, 1 tablespoon each mustard and balsamic vinegar and ½ teaspoon honey and pour over the salad.

 Chicken and Cashew Stir-Fry

Mix together 2 tablespoons cornflour, 150 ml (¼ pint) chicken stock, 3 tablespoons tamari soy sauce, ½ teaspoon ground ginger and ½ teaspoon chilli sauce. Heat 1 tablespoon vegetable oil in a wok over a high heat and stir-fry 500 g (1 lb) chicken breasts, cut into strips, for about 5 minutes. Remove the chicken from the wok and set aside. Add 1 chopped onion, 1 deseeded and chopped green pepper, 220 g (7½ oz) can water chestnuts, drained, and 100 g (3½ oz) cashew nuts to the pan and stir-fry for 5–6 minutes. Pour in the cornflour mixture and bring to the boil, stirring continuously. Add the reserved chicken and stir until the sauce thickens and the chicken is heated through. Sprinkle with chopped spring onions and serve with cooked basmati rice.

Leek and Cheese Macaroni

Serves 4

200 g (7 oz) gluten-free macaroni or other short pasta
275 g (9 oz) leeks, thinly sliced
40 g (1½ oz) butter
25 g (1 oz) plain gluten-free flour
250 ml (8 fl oz) milk
35 g (1¼oz) Cheddar cheese, grated
75 g (3 oz) single cream
75 g (3 oz) baby tomatoes, halved
75 g (3 oz) Gruyère cheese, grated
salt and pepper

- Cook the macaroni according to the pack instructions. Two minutes before the end of cooking time, add the leeks to the saucepan.

- Meanwhile, melt the butter in a small saucepan over a medium heat and stir in the flour to make a roux. Gradually whisk in the milk and continue to cook and stir until the sauce thickens.

- Take the sauce off the heat and stir in the Cheddar cheese and cream. Season with salt and pepper.

- Drain the pasta and leeks and return to the pan. Pour in the sauce and mix well, then pour the macaroni mixture into an ovenproof dish.

- Top with the baby tomatoes and the Gruyère cheese, then place under a preheated hot grill for 6–7 minutes, until golden and bubbling.

 Leek and Cheese Pizza

Toast 4 gluten-free pitta breads for 2 minutes on each side. Meanwhile, heat 1 tablespoon olive oil and 25 g (1 oz) butter in a frying pan, add 3 thinly sliced leeks and cook for 4–5 minutes, until tender. Top each pitta with cooked leeks and sprinkle over 12 chopped baby tomatoes and 150 g (5 oz) grated Gruyère and place under a preheated hot grill for 1–2 minutes, until golden and bubbling. Serve with a crisp green salad.

 Leek and Cheese Fusilli

Heat 1 tablespoon olive oil and 25 g (1 oz) butter in a frying pan over a medium heat. Cook 1 teaspoon dried chilli flakes for 1–2 minutes, then add 3 sliced leeks and cook for 6–7 minutes. Meanwhile, cook 350 g (11½ oz) gluten-free fusilli according to the pack instructions. Stir 12 halved baby tomatoes into the leeks. Drain the pasta and stir into the leeks. Pour into an ovenproof dish, top with 75 g (3 oz) grated Gruyère and place under a preheated hot grill for 3–4 minutes, until golden and bubbling. Serve with a crisp green salad.

 # Salmon Stew with Mashed Potato

Serves 4

1 tablespoon olive oil

1 onion, chopped

2 garlic cloves, crushed

1 teaspoon ground cumin

½ teaspoon paprika

400 g (13 oz) can chopped tomatoes

1 red pepper, deseeded and chopped

200 ml (7 fl oz) fish stock

875 g (1¾ lb) potatoes, peeled and chopped

500 g (1 lb) salmon fillets, cut into large chunks

125 g (4 oz) raw peeled king prawns

50 g (2 oz) unsalted butter

2 teaspoons creamed horseradish

small handful of chopped parsley

salt and pepper

- Heat the oil in a large saucepan over a medium heat, add the onion, garlic, cumin and paprika and cook for 3–4 minutes.

- Add the chopped tomatoes, red pepper and stock and bring to a simmer. Cook for 8–10 minutes.

- Meanwhile, cook the potatoes in boiling water for 12–15 minutes, until tender.

- Add the salmon and prawns to the tomato mixture and cook for 4–5 minutes.

- Drain the potatoes and mash with the butter, horseradish and some salt and pepper.

- Scatter the parsley over the salmon stew and spoon over the mash.

 Pan-Fried Salmon with Griddled Sweet Potatoes Boil 625 g (1¼ lb) peeled and thickly sliced sweet potatoes for 5 minutes, then drain and toss with 1–2 tablespoons olive oil. Cook the slices for 2–3 minutes on a hot griddle, until the edges start to caramelize. Meanwhile, pan-fry 4 x 150 g (5 oz) salmon fillets in 1 tablespoon oil for 2–3 minutes on each side, until cooked to your liking. Serve with a salad.

 Salmon Fish Cakes Heat 1 tablespoon olive oil in a frying pan over a medium heat, add 4 thinly sliced spring onions and cook for 3–4 minutes, then place in a bowl. Under a preheated hot grill, cook 200 g (7 oz) salmon fillets and 300 g (10 oz) cod fillets for 3–4 minutes one each side. Flake the fish and mix with the spring onions, 500 g (1 lb) ready-made mashed potatoes and 2 tablespoons chopped dill.

With wet hands, shape the fish mixture into 8 round cakes. Dust with 1–2 tablespoons plain gluten-free flour. Heat another 2 tablespoons olive oil in the frying pan and cook the fish cakes for 3–4 minutes on each side, until golden. Meanwhile, steam 300 g (10 oz) baby spinach leaves until wilted, and heat 300 ml (½ pint) ready-made cheese sauce. Serve the fish cakes on a bed of spinach with a drizzle of cheese sauce.

GLU-FAMI-NYK

10 Cheat's Pepper Pizza

Serves 4

4 gluten-free pitta breads

4 tablespoons tomato ketchup

4 ready-roasted red and yellow peppers from a jar, drained and sliced

4 spring onions, sliced

150 g (5 oz) mozzarella cheese, sliced

small handful of rocket leaves.

- Toast the pitta breads for 2 minutes on each side. Top each one with 1 tablespoon tomato ketchup and the roasted peppers, spring onions and mozzarella.

- Place under a preheated hot grill and cook for 4–6 minutes, until bubbling and golden. Serve topped with the rocket.

 Roast Pepper Pasta

Place 2 deseeded and halved red peppers and 2 deseeded and halved yellow peppers under a preheated hot grill and grill for 10–12 minutes, or until blackened. Place in a bowl, cover with clingfilm and leave until cool enough to handle. Meanwhile, cook 350 g (11½ oz) gluten-free pasta for 9–12 minutes, or according to the pack instructions. Peel the skin off the peppers and slice the flesh. Heat 1 tablespoon olive oil in a frying pan, add 2 sliced garlic cloves and cook for 1 minute, then add the peppers. Cook for 1 minute, then place the pepper mixture in a large bowl. Drain the pasta and add to the bowl with 4–5 torn basil leaves and a small handful of rocket leaves. Toss, sprinkle with grated Parmesan and serve immediately.

 Polenta Pepper Pizza

Bring 1 litre (1¾ pints) water to the boil in a large saucepan. Slowly pour in 250 g (8 oz) polenta, stirring constantly. Add 1 teaspoon dried oregano, season and continue to cook, stirring, for 8–10 minutes, until the polenta is thick. Divide in half, pour out onto 2 lightly oiled baking sheets, and spread into a circle about 1 cm (½ inch) thick. Bake in a preheated oven, 200°C (400°F), Gas Mark 6, for 12 minutes. Spread 400 g (13 oz) can chopped tomatoes over the polenta, then top with 350 g (11½ oz) ready-roasted peppers, cut into strips, and 10–12 roughly torn basil leaves, then sprinkle with 250 g (8 oz) sliced mozzarella. Bake for a further 12–15 minutes, until the cheese is golden and bubbling. Serve hot, cut into wedges.

30 Roast Duck Breast with Plum Sauce

Serves 4

4 duck breasts
1 tablespoon olive oil
2 shallots, diced
400 g (13 oz) ripe plums, stoned
 and cut into small wedges
75 g (3 oz) light muscovado sugar
2 sprigs thyme
2 star anise
100 ml (3½ fl oz) red wine
450 ml (¾ pint) beef stock
salt and pepper
steamed green vegetables,
 to serve

- Score the skin of the duck breasts with a sharp knife and season well with salt and pepper.

- Heat a nonstick, ovenproof saucepan over a medium heat, add the duck, skinside down, and cook for 6–7 minutes.

- Meanwhile, heat the oil in a saucepan, add the shallots and cook for 3–4 minutes. Add the plums and sugar and cook for a further 2–3 minutes until the sugar has dissolved.

- Turn the duck breasts over and add the thyme and star anise to the pan. Transfer to a preheated oven, 180°C (350°F), Gas Mark 4, and roast for 10–12 minutes.

- Meanwhile, add the wine and stock to the plums and simmer for 12–15 minutes, stirring occasionally.

- Remove the duck breasts from the oven and leave to rest for 5 minutes, then cut each one into slices.

- Divide the steamed vegetables between 4 warmed plates. Place the duck on top, with the plum sauce spooned over.

 Smoked Duck Breast and Plum Salad Toss together the seeds of 1 pomegranate, 4 tablespoons toasted flaked almonds, 2 plums, stoned and cut into thin wedges, the leaves of 1 small frisée lettuce and 2 tablespoons chopped chives with a ready-made salad dressing of your choice. Divide the salad between 4 plates. Cut 2 smoked duck breasts into slices and place on top of the salad.

 Duck Breast with Plum Sauce and Crushed Potatoes Cook 600 g (1¼lb) new potatoes in boiling water for 12–15 minutes until tender, adding 100 g (3½ oz) trimmed and halved green beans 3 minutes from the end of cooking time. Meanwhile, make the plum sauce as above. Score the skin of 4 duck breasts and season with salt and pepper. Heat a nonstick ovenproof frying pan over a medium heat, add the duck breasts, skinside down, and cook for 5 minutes until golden.

Turn over the duck breasts, transfer the pan to a preheated oven, 190°C (375°F), Gas Mark 5, and cook for a further 3– 4 minutes. Remove from the oven and leave to rest for 5 minutes, then slice. Drain the potatoes and beans and return to the pan with 25 g (1 oz) butter and 2 tablespoons chopped chives. Lightly crush the potatoes, then divide them between 4 warmed plates. Top with the sliced duck and pour over the plum sauce to serve.

 # Tagliatelle with Dolcelatte and Walnut Sauce

Serves 4

350 g (11½ oz) gluten-free
  tagliatelle
250 ml (8 fl oz) single cream
200 g (7 oz) dolcelatte cheese,
  crumbled
100 g (3½ oz) walnut pieces,
  toasted
2 tablespoons shredded basil
  leaves

- Cook the pasta in a large saucepan of boiling water for 8–9 minutes, or according to the pack instructions.

- Meanwhile, put the single cream in a frying pan with the dolcelatte and place over a medium-low heat. When the cheese is melted, stir in the walnuts.

- Drain the pasta and toss in the creamy cheese and walnut sauce.

- Serve in warmed bowls, sprinkled with the shredded basil.

 ### Dolcelatte and Walnut Tortilla

Pizza Wilt 300 g (10 oz) baby spinach leaves in a saucepan with 1 tablespoon olive oil. Heat 2 gluten-free tortillas according to the pack instructions. Place the tortillas on baking sheets and spread with a 200 g (7 oz) can chopped tomatoes. Sprinkle with 200 g (7 oz) crumbled dolcelatte and 100 g (3½ oz) toasted walnut pieces. Toast under a preheated hot grill for 3–4 minutes, until bubbling and golden.

 ### Dolcelatte and Tomato Pizza

Heat 1 tablespoon olive oil in a saucepan, add 3 sliced garlic cloves and 1 chopped small onion and cook for 3–4 minutes. Stir in a 400 g (13 oz) can of chopped tomatoes and 6–8 torn basil leaves and cook for a further 3–4 minutes. Place 2 gluten-free pizza bases on a baking sheet and spoon over the tomato sauce, spreading it to the edges. Top with 40 g (1¾ oz) roughly chopped watercress and 4 sliced tomatoes. Thinly slice ½ red onion and sprinkle over the tomatoes, then crumble over 200 g (7 oz) dolcelatte and top with 2 tablespoons pine nuts. Bake in a preheated oven, 220°C (425°F), Gas Mark 7, for 20–22 minutes, until golden and bubbling. Serve with a crisp green salad.

Mackerel Curry

Serves 4

1 green chilli, deseeded and
  chopped
1 teaspoon ground coriander
½ teaspoon turmeric
4 garlic cloves
2.5 cm (1 inch) piece of fresh root
  ginger, peeled and sliced
1 teaspoon sunflower oil
1 tablespoon coconut oil
1 teaspoon cumin seeds
1 large onion, sliced
150 ml (¼ pint) coconut milk
450 g (14½ oz) mackerel fillets,
  cut into 5 cm (2 inch) pieces
small handful of coriander leaves,
  roughly torn
salt and pepper

- Place the chilli, ground coriander, turmeric, garlic, ginger and sunflower oil in a small blender and blend together to make a smooth paste.

- Heat the coconut oil in a wok or frying pan over a medium heat, add the spice paste and the cumin and cook for 2–3 minutes.

- Add the onion to the pan and cook for 1–2 minutes, then pour in the coconut milk and 250 ml (8 fl oz) water. Bring to the boil, then simmer for 5 minutes. Season with salt and pepper.

- Add the mackerel pieces to the pan and cook for 6–8 minutes until the fish is cooked, then stir in the coriander leaves.

 Mackerel and Orange Cumin Couscous Salad Cover 250 g (8 oz) couscous with boiling water and leave to stand for 8 minutes. Segment 2 oranges and break 4 smoked mackerel fillets into large flakes. Whisk together 3 tablespoons olive oil, 4 tablespoons lemon juice, 1 teaspoon each honey and Dijon mustard and ½ teaspoon ground cumin. Fluff up the couscous with a fork and stir in the orange segments, fish, ½ chopped cucumber, 2 tablespoons chopped parsley, 50 g (2 oz) watercress and the dressing.

Cumin Beetroot with Mackerel and Horseradish Cut 425 g (14 oz) beetroot into 4–6 wedges, place in a roasting tin with 2 tablespoons olive oil, 2 teaspoons cumin seeds, 2 tablespoons thyme and 2 teaspoons clear honey and mix to coat. Roast in a preheated oven, 200°C (400°F), Gas Mark 6, for 25 minutes. Meanwhile, whisk together 2 tablespoons creamed horseradish, 4 tablespoons lemon juice and 150 ml (¼ pint) natural yogurt. Heat 4 smoked mackerel fillets according to the pack instructions and flake into large flakes. Place a few small handfuls of baby spinach leaves onto 4 plates and scatter over the mackerel and beetroot. Sprinkle with the horseradish dressing and serve.

30 Spiced Shepherd's Pie

Serves 4

2 tablespoons olive oil
500 g (1 lb) minced lamb
1 large onion, chopped
2 carrots, peeled and diced
2 garlic cloves, chopped
1 teaspoon ground cumin
½ teaspoon ground cinnamon
½ teaspoon mixed spice
250 ml (8 fl oz) lamb stock
4 tablespoons tomato purée
1 teaspoon dark muscovado sugar
875 g (1¾ lb) sweet potatoes,
  peeled and chopped
25 g (1 oz) butter
1 tablespoon chopped coriander
  leaves
salt and pepper

- Heat the oil in a saucepan over a medium heat, add the lamb and brown for 3–4 minutes, then remove from the pan.

- Add the onion, carrots and garlic to the pan and cook for 2–3 minutes, then stir in the spices. Return the lamb to the pan and stir to coat with the spices. Pour in the stock, stir in the tomato purée and sugar and simmer for 12 minutes, stirring occasionally.

- Meanwhile, cook the sweet potatoes in a large saucepan of boiling water for 12–15 minutes until tender. Drain and mash with the butter and salt and pepper.

- Stir the chopped coriander into the lamb, spoon into an ovenproof dish and top with the mashed sweet potato.

- Bake in a preheated oven, 200°C (400°F), Gas Mark 6, for 10–12 minutes and serve.

Spiced Lamb Kebabs

Mix 450 g (14½ oz) minced lamb with 2 tablespoons lemon juice. In a blender, blend together 1 tablespoon olive oil, 50 g (2 oz) coriander leaves, 2 deseeded and chopped green chillies, 4 crushed garlic cloves, 1 teaspoon ground cumin, ½ teaspoon each ground coriander, turmeric and garam masala and 2 teaspoons grated fresh root ginger. Mix the paste into the lamb and squeeze the mixture onto 8 skewers. Brush each kebab with olive oil and grill for 2–3 minutes on each side, or until cooked through.

Spiced Lamb Chops with Chickpea and Red Pepper Salad

In a large bowl, mix together 4 tablespoons lemon juice, 2 teaspoons ground cumin and 1 teaspoon paprika. Add 8 lamb loin chops, rub the spice mixture over the meat and leave to marinate for 5 minutes. Heat a griddle pan and cook the lamb for 3–4 minutes on each side, then leave to rest for 5 minutes. Meanwhile, mix together a 400 g (13 oz) can chickpeas, rinsed and drained, and 125 g (4 oz) sliced ready-roasted red peppers in a bowl. Heat 2 tablespoons olive oil in a frying pan, add 1 thinly sliced red onion and cook for 2–3 minutes. Add 2 sliced garlic cloves and cook for a further minute, then pour in 2 tablespoons red wine vinegar. Pour over the chickpea mixture and stir in with 2 tablespoons chopped coriander leaves. Divide the salad between 4 plates and top each one with 2 lamb chops.

GLU-FAMI-BIO

30 Mushroom Risotto

Serves 4

50 g (2 oz) dried porcini

1 litre (1¾ pints) hot vegetable stock

1 tablespoon olive oil

50 g (2 oz) unsalted butter

100 g (3½ oz) chestnut mushrooms, sliced

1 garlic clove, crushed

3 shallots, chopped

300 g (10 oz) Arborio risotto rice

75 ml (3 fl oz) white wine

125 g (4 oz) Parmesan cheese, grated

- Place the dried porcini in a small bowl and cover with some of the stock. Leave to stand for 10 minutes. Keep the remaining stock warm over a low heat.

- Heat the oil and butter in a saucepan over a medium heat, add the mushrooms, garlic and shallots and cook for 2–3 minutes.

- Add the rice and stir until well coated, then pour in the wine and let it bubble until it has all been absorbed by the rice.

- Add a ladle of the hot stock to the pan and cook, stirring, until all the stock has been absorbed. Repeat this process until the rice is tender, but still has a slight bite.

- Remove the porcini from the stock and roughly chop, then stir into the risotto with 75 g (3 oz) of the grated Parmesan.

- Serve with the remaining Parmesan sprinkled over the top.

 Portobello Mushrooms with Mushroom Risotto Heat 500 g (1 lb) ready-made mushroom risotto according to the pack instructions. Meanwhile, place 4 large portobello mushrooms on a baking sheet and sprinkle with 2 teaspoons chopped thyme leaves and 2 tablespoons olive oil. Place under a preheated grill and cook for 8 minutes. Spoon the risotto into the mushrooms and serve sprinkled with 2 tablespoons grated Parmesan.

 Mushroom and Rice Pot Heat 1 tablespoon olive oil in a saucepan over a medium heat, add 1 large chopped onion, 250 g (8 oz) sliced mushrooms, 2 tablespoons chopped thyme and 2 deseeded and sliced red peppers and cook for 3–4 minutes. Stir in 200 g (7 oz) basmati rice, a 400 g (13 oz) can chopped tomatoes and 425 ml (14½ fl oz) vegetable stock and some salt and pepper. Bring to the boil, then cover and simmer for 17–18 minutes, until the rice is cooked. Scatter with 2 tablespoons chopped parsley to serve.

Spaghetti Arrabiata with Chilli and Prawns

Serves 4

350 g (11½ oz) gluten-free spaghetti
3 tablespoons olive oil
½ red chilli, diced
4 garlic cloves, crushed
1 kg (2 lb) ripe tomatoes, skinned
2 tablespoons lemon juice
½ teaspoon caster sugar
250 g (8 oz) tiger or jumbo prawns, cooked and peeled
small handful of basil, roughly torn
Parmesan cheese shavings, to serve

- Cook the spaghetti in a large saucepan of boiling water for 8–9 minutes, according to the pack instructions, until 'al dente'.

- Meanwhile, heat the oil in a frying pan over a medium heat, add red chilli and garlic and cook for 1–2 minutes.

- Add the tomatoes, lemon juice and sugar and cook for a further 6–7 minutes, adding the prawns for the last minute of cooking time.

- Drain the pasta and toss in the arrabiata sauce. Stir in the torn basil.

- Serve sprinkled with Parmesan shavings.

 Chilli Prawn Stir-Fry

Cook 150 g (5 oz) rice noodles according to the pack instructions. Drain and toss with 1 teaspoon sesame oil. Heat 2 teaspoons oil in a wok, stir-fry 2 deseeded and diced red chillies, 2 teaspoons grated root ginger and 3 crushed garlic cloves for 1 minute, then add 1 chopped red pepper, 125 g (4 oz) broccoli florets, 4 sliced spring onions, 12 halved baby tomatoes and 200 g (7 oz) raw peeled tiger prawns. Cook for 4–5 minutes until the prawns are pink, then add the noodles, 2 sliced pak choi, 1 tablespoon tamari soy sauce and 2 tablespoons sweet chilli sauce. Cook for a further 3–4 minutes.

 Tomato and Chilli Prawn Pizza

Put 400 g (13 oz) plain gluten-free flour, ½ teaspoon salt, 2 tablespoons olive oil, 7 g sachet fast-action dried yeast and some salt and pepper into a food processor and process until well mixed. With the machine running, gradually add a little water to make a soft dough. Tip onto a work surface and knead until the dough comes together. Divide into 4 and roll out each piece to a very thin 25 cm (10 inch) circle. Place each one on a lightly oiled baking sheet. Mix together a 400 g (13 oz) can chopped tomatoes, 2 crushed garlic cloves and ½ diced red chilli. Spread the mixture over the pizza bases and top with 250 g (8 oz) cooked peeled tiger or jumbo prawns, some torn basil leaves and 250 g (8 oz) sliced mozzarella. Bake in a preheated oven, 220°C (425°F) Gas Mark 7, for 12–15 minutes. Cut into wedges to serve.

30 Fish Pie

Serves 4

350 ml (12 fl oz) milk

125 g (4½ oz) salmon fillet, cut into bite-sized pieces

375 g (13 oz) cod loin or fillet, cut into bite-sized pieces

75 g (3 oz) baby spinach leaves

2 eggs

240 g (7½ oz) raw peeled king prawns

20 g (¾ oz) butter

1 tablespoon plain gluten-free flour

½ teaspoon mustard

675 g (1 lb 5 oz) sweet potatoes, peeled and chopped

50 g (2 oz) Cheddar cheese, grated

salt and pepper

- Place the milk in a saucepan over a medium heat and add the salmon and cod. Bring to a simmer and cook for 5–6 minutes. Drain the fish, reserving the milk.

- Put the spinach in an ovenproof dish and top with the fish.

- Boil the eggs for 3 minutes until just softly boiled, then peel and cut into quarters and place on top of the fish. Scatter the prawns around the dish.

- Melt the butter in a small saucepan over a medium heat and stir in the flour to make a roux. Stir in the mustard, then gradually add the reserved milk, whisking continuously until you have a thick and creamy sauce. Pour over the fish.

- Cook the sweet potatoes in a pan of boiling water for 12-15 minutes until tender, then drain and mash with plenty of pepper. Spoon the potato over the fish pie, then use a fork to spread it around in attractive patterns. Top with the Cheddar.

- Bake in a preheated oven, 200°C (400°F), Gas Mark 6, for 15–18 minutes.

10 Potato Topped with Fish and Egg

Heat 500 g (1 lb) ready-made mashed potato in a microwave. Grill 4 x 150 g (5 oz) cod loins for 3–4 minutes on each side, until cooked through. Meanwhile, poach 4 eggs. Stir 2 tablespoons chopped chives through the mash and divide between 4 plates. Top each with a cod fillet and a poached egg, then spoon over 2 tablespoons ready-made warmed cheese sauce.

20 Quick Fish Pie

Place 350 g (11½ oz) salmon fillet and 250 g (8 oz) cod fillet under a preheated grill and grill for 4–5 minutes on each side, then cut into chunks and place in an ovenproof dish. Meanwhile, boil 3 eggs for 8–9 minutes. Refresh the hard-boiled eggs under cold running water, then peel, cut in half and place in the ovenproof dish with the fish. Sprinkle over 100 g (3½ oz) frozen peas. Mix together 2 tablespoons smooth mustard, 2 tablespoons chopped chives and 300 g (10 oz) natural yogurt and pour over the fish. Top with 750 g (1½ lb) ready-made mashed potato and sprinkle over 75 g (3 oz) grated Cheddar. Bake in a preheated oven, 200°C (400°F), Gas Mark 6, for 10 minutes.

30 Cheese Roulade with Spinach and Walnuts

Serves 4

30 g (1¼ oz) unsalted butter

30 g (1¼ oz) plain gluten-free flour

200 ml (7 fl oz) milk

pinch of cayenne pepper

4 large eggs, separated

2 teaspoons Dijon mustard

85 g (3¾ oz) Cheddar cheese, grated

50 g (2 oz) walnuts, finely chopped

200 g (7 oz) cream cheese

100 g (3½ oz) baby spinach leaves

3 finely sliced spring onions

salt and pepper

- Melt the butter in a small saucepan over a medium heat. Grease a 33 x 23 cm (13 x 9 inch) Swiss roll tin with a little of the melted butter, then line it with baking paper.

- Stir the flour into the remaining melted butter to make a roux. Gradually whisk in the milk and continue to cook until the sauce comes to the boil and is thick and creamy. Remove from the heat, add the cayenne and season. Stir in the egg yolks, mustard, Cheddar and 40 g (1¾ oz) of the walnuts.

- In a large grease-free bowl, whisk the egg whites with a hand-held electric whisk until stiff peaks form. Fold the egg whites into the cheese mixture and gently pour into the prepared tin. Bake in a preheated oven, 200°C (400°F), Gas Mark 6, for 10–12 minutes, until firm to the touch.

- Sprinkle the remaining walnuts onto a piece of baking paper slightly larger than the tin. Turn the roulade out onto the paper, peel off the lining paper and use the paper to gently roll it up. Cover with a damp cloth and leave to cool slightly.

- Unroll the roulade, spread with the cream cheese and sprinkle over the spinach and spring onions, then re-roll. Serve warm or cold.

 Spinach and Walnut Salad

Dry-fry 30 g (1¼ oz) chopped walnuts for 2–3 minutes. Whisk together 3 tablespoons olive oil, 2 tablespoons lemon juice and ½ teaspoon each honey and mustard. Toss 100 g (3½ oz) baby spinach with 4 sliced spring onions, ½ chopped cucumber, 4 sliced tomatoes and the nuts. Crumble over 150 g (5 oz) goats' cheese. Pour over the dressing.

 Spinach and Walnut Pasta

Dry-fry 50 g (2 oz) walnuts for 2–3 minutes, then place them in a food processor with 1 chopped garlic clove, 25 g (1 oz) grated Parmesan, 40 g (1¾ oz) baby spinach leaves and 2 tablespoons lemon juice. Process until everything is broken up. With the food processor running, gradually pour in 50–75 ml (2–3 fl oz) extra virgin olive oil, until the pesto is the consistency you want. Cook 350 g (11½ oz) gluten-free pasta in a large pan of boiling water for 10–12 minutes, or according to the pack instructions. Drain the pasta and toss with the pesto. Serve sprinkled with Parmesan shavings.

Crab and Mussel Tagliatelle

Serves 4

2 tablespoons olive oil

1 onion, chopped

2 garlic cloves, crushed

400 g (13 oz) can chopped tomatoes

150 ml (¼ pint) white wine

1 red chilli, deseeded and diced

375 g (12 oz) gluten-free tagliatelle

400 g (13 oz) mussels, cleaned

250 g (8 oz) crab meat (white and dark)

4 tablespoons lemon juice

small handful of parsley, chopped

salt and pepper

- Heat the oil in a frying pan over a medium heat, add the onion and garlic and cook for 3–4 minutes. Add the chopped tomatoes, white wine and chilli, season with salt and pepper and simmer for 8–9 minutes.

- Cook the tagliatelle in a large pan of boiling water for 9–12 minutes, or according to the pack instructions.

- Meanwhile, add the mussels to the tomato sauce, cover and cook for 4 minutes, until all the shells are open (discard any mussels that do not open).

- Drain the tagliatelle and stir into the tomato sauce with the crab meat, lemon juice and parsley. Mix well and serve immediately.

 Crab and Smoked Mussel Quinoa Salad Place 125 g (4 oz) quinoa in a pan with 500 ml (17 fl oz) water and cook over a medium heat for 8–9 minutes, until all the water has been absorbed or the quinoa is cooked. Drain the quinoa and place in a bowl with 200 g (7 oz) crab meat (white and dark), 200 g (7 oz) smoked mussels, 1 tablespoon chopped parsley, ½ tablespoon chopped basil, 4 diced tomatoes, ½ diced cucumber, 4 tablespoons lemon juice and 1 tablespoon extra virgin olive oil. Mix well and serve on a bed of salad leaves.

 Crab and Mussel Penne Bake Cook 300 g (10 oz) gluten-free penne in boiling water for 9–12 minutes, or according to the pack instructions. Meanwhile, heat 1 tablespoon olive oil in a pan over a medium heat, add 1 thinly sliced leek, 1 peeled and finely diced carrot, 1 diced celery stick and 2 crushed garlic cloves and cook for 4–5 minutes, until softened. Stir in 2 x 400 g (13 oz) cans of chopped tomatoes and 2 tablespoons shredded basil leaves and cook for 8–10 minutes. Stir in the cooked and drained pasta, 200 g (7 oz) dark and white crab meat and 100 g (3½ oz) shelled mussels. Pour into an ovenproof dish and sprinkle with 100 g (3½ oz) grated Emmental. Cook under a preheated grill for 8–10 minutes, until golden and bubbling. Serve immediately.

30 Creamy Herb-Stuffed Chicken Breast

Serves 4

4 skinless chicken breasts
150 g (5 oz) cream cheese
2 garlic cloves, crushed
½ tablespoon chopped parsley
½ tablespoon chopped chives
10 slices of Parma ham
½ tablespoon vegetable oil,
   for oiling
2 leeks, finely sliced
300 ml (½ pint) fromage frais
salt and pepper
crisp green salad, to serve

- Using a sharp knife, make a slit in the side of each chicken breast, to make a little pocket.

- Mix together the cream cheese, garlic, herbs and some salt and pepper.

- Lay 2 slices of the Parma ham on a cutting board and place one of the chicken breasts on top. Spoon one-quarter of the cream cheese mixture into the chicken breast, then wrap around the Parma ham to seal the pocket. Repeat with the remaining ham, cream cheese and chicken to give 4 parcels. Place in a roasting tin and bake in a preheated oven, 200°C (400°F), Gas Mark 6, for 25 minutes.

- Meanwhile, chop the remaining Parma ham and fry in a lightly oiled frying pan over a medium heat for 1–2 minutes. Add the leeks and stir-fry for 2–3 minutes, then stir in the fromage frais and some salt and pepper.

- Serve the chicken with a crisp green salad and the bacon and leek sauce.

 Herby Chicken Pittas

Mix 150 g (5 oz) cream cheese with 2 tablespoons chopped fresh herbs of your choice. Toast 4 gluten-free pitta breads for 2–3 minutes on each side, then cut along the long side to open like a pocket. Spread the inside of each pitta bread with cream cheese. Slice 3 ready-cooked chicken breasts, then stuff each pitta bread with one-quarter of the chicken, 30 g (1¼ oz) crisp salad leaves and a dollop of mango sauce.

 Lemon Chicken with Herb Quinoa

Cook 150 g (5 oz) quinoa in twice its volume of boiling water for 9–10 minutes, or according to the pack instructions. Meanwhile, drizzle 4 tablespoons lemon juice over 4 chicken breasts, season with salt and pepper, then cook on a hot griddle for 5–7 minutes on each side until cooked through. Drain the quinoa and stir in 2 tablespoons chopped parsley, 1 tablespoon chopped chives, ½ tablespoon chopped mint and 2 diced tomatoes.

Serve the chicken on a bed of the herb quinoa.

Mint-Crusted Lamb Cutlets with Pea Mash

Serves 4

750 g (1½ lb) new potatoes, halved if large
150 g (5 oz) peas, frozen or fresh
1 tablespoon olive oil
2 French-trimmed racks of lamb
100 g (3½ oz) gluten-free breadcrumbs
2 tablespoons freshly chopped mint
2 tablespoons Dijon mustard
25 g (1 oz) butter
1 tablespoon crème fraîche
salt and pepper
redcurrant jelly, to serve

- Cook the potatoes in boiling water for 12–15 minutes, until tender. Meanwhile, cook the peas in boiling water for 3 minutes until tender.

- Heat 1 tablespoon of the oil in a frying pan over a medium heat, add the lamb and brown on all sides for 2–3 minutes. Remove the lamb from the pan and place on a baking sheet.

- Mix together the breadcrumbs and mint and season with salt and pepper.

- Spread the fat side of each rack with the mustard and then press on the breadcrumb mixture. Sprinkle with the remaining oil and bake in a preheated oven, 200°C (400°F), Gas Mark 6, for 12–15 minutes, until golden (or longer if you prefer your lamb less pink).

- Drain the potatoes and peas, then mash with the butter and crème fraîche. Season well with salt and pepper.

- Remove the lamb from the oven and cut each rack in half.

- Divide the mash between 4 warmed plates and top with the lamb. Serve with redcurrant jelly.

Lamb, Pea and Mint Salad

Grill 8 lamb cutlets for 3–4 minutes on each side. Meanwhile, toss together 150 g (5 oz) each peas and sugarsnap peas, 100 g (3½ oz) pea shoots, 150 g (5 oz) crumbled feta and a small handful of mint leaves. Whisk together 3 tablespoons olive oil, 1 tablespoon white wine vinegar and ½ teaspoon each Dijon mustard and honey. Drizzle over the salad and serve with the lamb.

Pea and Mint Risotto with Lamb Chops

Heat 1 litre (1¾ pints) vegetable stock. Meanwhile, melt 50 g (2 oz) butter in a heavy-based pan, add 4 sliced spring onions and cook for 2–3 minutes, then stir in 175 g (6 oz) Arborio risotto rice. Pour in 100 ml (3½ fl oz) white wine and cook, stirring, until it has been absorbed. Add a ladle of the stock and cook, stirring, until it has been absorbed. Repeat this step until the rice is tender, but with a slight bite. Meanwhile, cook 175 g (6 oz) frozen peas in boiling water for 3 minutes, then drain and lightly crush with 2 tablespoons chopped mint. Grill 4 lamb chops for 4–5 minutes on each side. When the risotto is cooked, stir in the minted peas and 2 tablespoons grated Parmesan. Season with salt and pepper. Serve the lamb chops on a bed of risotto, sprinkled with 2 tablespoons of toasted pine nuts.

30 Pasta with Pesto and Roast Vegetables

Serves 4

1 red pepper, deseeded and chopped

1 yellow pepper, deseeded and chopped

1 red onion, cut into wedges

2 courgettes, sliced

2 carrots, peeled and sliced

2 garlic cloves, sliced

8 baby tomatoes

2 tablespoons olive oil

2 teaspoons cumin seeds

275 g (9 oz) gluten-free pasta shapes

75 g (3 oz) pitted black olives

2 tablespoons pesto sauce

small handful of basil leaves, torn

salt and pepper

Parmesan cheese shavings, to serve

- Place all the vegetables, garlic and tomatoes in a large roasting tin and sprinkle with the oil, cumin seeds and some salt and pepper. Roast in a preheated oven, 200°C (400°F), Gas Mark 6, for 26–28 minutes.

- Halfway through the cooking time, bring a large pan of water to the boil and cook the pasta for 9–12 minutes, or according to the pack instructions, until 'al dente'.

- Drain the pasta and toss in the roasted vegetables, olives, pesto sauce and basil leaves.

- Serve sprinkled with Parmesan shavings.

Pasta and Vegetable Salad

Cook 350 g (11½ oz) gluten-free pasta in boiling water for 8–9 minutes. Meanwhile, in another pan of boiling water, blanch 125 g (4 oz) sugarsnap peas, 125 g (4 oz) trimmed green beans and 125 g (4 oz) peas for 3 minutes. Drain and refresh under cold running water. Drain the pasta, then toss with the vegetables, 2 tablespoons pesto sauce, 150 g (5 oz) crumbled feta, 25 g (1 oz) rocket leaves and 2 tablespoons toasted pine nuts.

Roast Vegetable Cheat's Pizza

Heat 1 tablespoon olive oil in a frying pan over a medium heat, add 1 deseeded and chopped red pepper, 1 deseeded and chopped yellow pepper, 2 thickly sliced red onions, 2 sliced garlic cloves and 2 sliced courgettes and cook for 10–12 minutes, stirring occasionally. Toast 4 gluten-free pitta breads and spread with 2 tablespoons pesto sauce. Spoon over the cooked vegetables and top with 200 g (7 oz) sliced mozzarella. Cook under a preheated hot grill for 4–5 minutes, until the cheese is melted and bubbling.

30 Mediterranean Olive Chicken

Serves 4

4 x 150 g (5 oz) chicken breasts
½ teaspoon paprika
1 tablespoon olive oil
1 red pepper, deseeded and chopped
1 red onion, chopped
1 garlic clove, crushed
400 g (13 oz) can chopped tomatoes
100 g (3½ oz) frozen spinach, defrosted
2 tablespoons green olives
1 teaspoon capers
1 tablespoon chopped basil

- Dust the chicken breasts with the paprika and cook on a hot griddle for 4–5 minutes on each side, then place in an ovenproof dish.

- Meanwhile, heat the oil in a pan over a medium heat, add the pepper, onion and garlic and cook for 3–4 minutes. Add the chopped tomatoes, spinach, olives, capers and basil and bring to a simmer. Season to taste with salt and pepper.

- Pour the sauce over the chicken and bake in a preheated oven, 200°C (400°F), Gas Mark 6, for 15–18 minutes, until the chicken is cooked through.

 1 **Mediterranean Chicken Olive Pittas** Toast 4 gluten-free pitta breads for 2–3 minutes on each side, then cut along the long side to open like a pocket. Slice 3 ready-cooked chicken breasts. Stuff each pitta with one-quarter of the chicken, a small handful of baby spinach leaves, 3–4 halved olives and 2–3 teaspoons tomato salsa.

 2 **Chicken Kebabs with Tomato and Olive Salsa** Cut 4 x 150 g (5 oz) skinless chicken breasts into bite-sized pieces and toss in a bowl with the grated rind of 1 lemon, 1 tablespoon chopped basil and 1 crushed garlic clove. Thread onto 8 skewers, presoaked in cold water to prevent burning, with 1 deseeded and chopped red pepper and 1 deseeded and chopped yellow pepper. Cook under a preheated hot grill for 15–16 minutes, turning occasionally. Meanwhile, mix together 6 diced ripe tomatoes, 1 diced shallot, 6–8 pitted and diced olives, 1 teaspoon lemon juice, 2 tablespoons olive oil and 1 tablespoon shredded basil. Serve the cooked kebabs with the salsa.

30 Spicy Lamb Tagine

Serves 4

2 tablespoons olive oil

750 g (1½ lb) shoulder of lamb, cut into cubes

1 onion, chopped

1 garlic clove, crushed

1 teaspoon ground cumin

1 teaspoon ground cinnamon

½ teaspoon ground ginger

500 ml (17 fl oz) chicken stock

2 tablespoons tomato purée

1 teaspoon soft dark brown sugar

75 g (3 oz) dried apricots

50 g (2 oz) prunes

50 g (2 oz) flaked almonds, toasted

cooked quinoa, to serve

- Heat the oil in a large casserole over a medium heat and brown the meat (you may have to do this in batches), then remove with a slotted spoon and set aside.

- Add the onion and garlic to the pan and cook for 2–3 minutes, then stir in the spices and cook for a further minute.

- Return the lamb to the pan with the stock, tomato purée, sugar and dried fruit. Bring to the boil, then simmer for 25 minutes.

- Serve sprinkled with toasted flaked almonds, with cooked quinoa.

 Spiced Lamb Chops with Quinoa Salad

Cook 100 g (3½ oz) quinoa in boiling water for 8–9 minutes. Mix together 2 teaspoons each turmeric, ground cumin and ground cinnamon and 1 teaspoon ground ginger. Rub the spice mixture over 4 x 150 g (5 oz) lamb chops, then cook on a hot griddle for 3–4 minutes on each side. Meanwhile, mix together 2 tablespoons chopped parsley, 1 tablespoon chopped mint, 50 g (2 oz) chopped dried apricots and 2 tablespoons toasted flaked almonds. Drain the quinoa, then stir in the herb mixture and serve with the lamb chops.

 Spiced Lamb Burgers

Mix together 1 small diced onion, 1 tablespoon grated fresh root ginger, 3 crushed garlic cloves, 10 g (½ oz) chopped coriander leaves, 1 deseeded and diced red chilli, 1 egg, ½ teaspoon ground cumin, some salt and pepper and 400 g (13 oz) minced lamb. Shape the mixture into 4 burgers and chill for 6–8 minutes. Meanwhile, make the quinoa salad as in the recipe left. Heat 1 tablespoon olive oil in a frying pan and cook the burgers for 4–5 minutes on each side. Serve with the quinoa salad, a dollop of natural yogurt and sprinkling of paprika.

Pan-Fried Red Mullet with Fennel Mash

Serves 4

625 g (1¼ lb) peeled and diced potatoes
2 fennel bulbs, trimmed and diced
1 tablespoon olive oil
8 x 100 g (3½ oz) red mullet fillets
25 g (1 oz) butter
1 tablespoon chopped parsley
watercress sprigs, to serve

- Cook the potatoes and fennel in a pan of boiling water for 8–9 minutes, until tender.

- Meanwhile, heat the oil in a pan over a medium heat, add the red mullet fillets and cook for 2–3 minutes on each side.

- Drain the potato and fennel and roughly mash with the butter and chopped parsley. Serve the red mullet on a bed of the mash with a few watercress sprigs.

 Marinated Red Mullet with Leeks

Cut 3 slices into each side of 4 whole red mullet. Sprinkle with 2 tablespoons olive oil, 3 tablespoons lime juice and 1 tablespoon fennel seeds and leave to marinate for 10 minutes. Meanwhile, heat 1 tablespoon olive oil in a frying pan over a medium heat, add 3 sliced leeks and cook for 5–6 minutes, until softened. Stir in 3 skinned and chopped tomatoes and simmer for 4–5 minutes. Leave to cool for a few minutes. Spoon the leek mixture into the cavity of the fish. Cook under a preheated medium grill for 7–8 minutes on each side, until cooked through. Serve with steamed green vegetables and mashed potatoes.

 Steamed Red Mullet and Leeks with Fennel Mash Cut 8 pieces of greaseproof paper into squares large enough to cover a red mullet fillet, plus a 3.5 cm (1½ inch) border. Lightly brush 4 of the squares with a little oil and place on a baking sheet. Divide 300 g (10 oz) baby spinach leaves and 2 sliced leeks between the 4 oiled squares, then add 1 tablespoon crème fraîche, a splash of white wine, 2 red mullet fillets, 2 slices of lime and some salt and pepper to each one. Top with the remaining squares of greaseproof paper and fold up the edges to form parcels. Bake in a preheated oven, 200°C (400°F), Gas Mark 6, for 15–20 minutes.

Meanwhile, cook 2 trimmed and chopped fennel bulbs and 625 g (1¼ lb) peeled and diced potatoes in a pan of boiling water until tender. Drain and mash. Stir in 25 g (1 oz) butter and 1 tablespoon chopped parsley. Serve the fish and vegetables over a bed of fennel mash.

30 Ratatouille Pizza

Serves 4

2 x 400 g (13 oz) cans ratatouille
2 crushed garlic cloves
4 tablespoons tomato purée
6–8 basil leaves, roughly torn
4 x gluten-free pizza bases
125 g (4 oz) grated mozzarella
   cheese
drizzle of olive oil
salt and pepper

- Mix together the ratatouille, garlic, tomato purée and basil leaves and season with salt and pepper.

- Place the pizza bases on 2 baking sheets, then spoon over the ratatouille mixture.

- Sprinkle over the grated mozzarella, drizzle with the oil and bake in a preheated oven, 220°C (425°F), Gas Mark 7, for 25 minutes, until hot and bubbling.

 Ratatouille Pasta
Cook 350 g (11½ oz) gluten-free pasta in a saucepan of boiling water for 8–9 minutes, until 'al dente'. Meanwhile, heat a 400 g (13 oz) can of ratatouille in a saucepan with 2 crushed garlic cloves, 6–8 torn basil leaves and a drizzle of olive oil. Drain the pasta and toss in the ratatouille. Serve sprinkled with 2–3 tablespoons grated Parmesan.

 Ratatouille Pitta Pizza
Heat 1 tablespoon olive oil in a saucepan over a medium heat, add 1 chopped red onion, 2 chopped garlic cloves, 1 deseeded and chopped red pepper, 1 deseeded and chopped yellow pepper and 2 sliced courgettes and cook for 3–4 minutes. Stir in a 400 g (13 oz) can of chopped tomatoes, 6–8 roughly torn basil leaves and some salt and pepper. Grill 4 gluten-free pitta breads for 2 minutes on each side. Place the pittas on a baking sheet and spoon over the ratatouille. Top with 150 g (5 oz) grated mozzarella and cook under the hot grill for 3–4 minutes, until the cheese is golden and bubbling.

Thai Chicken Meatballs with Noodles

Serves 4

500 g (1 lb) minced chicken
3 spring onions, finely diced
2 garlic cloves, finely diced
1 red chilli, deseeded and finely
 diced
5 cm (2 inch) piece of fresh root
 ginger, peeled and finely diced
600 ml (1 pint) chicken stock
350 g (11½ oz) rice noodles
300 g (10 oz) ready-made
 tomato sauce, heated
coriander leaves, to garnish

- Mix together the minced chicken, spring onions, garlic, chilli and ginger. Using wet hands, divide the chicken mixture into 16 portions and roll into balls.

- Pour the stock into a large pan and bring to the boil. Add the meatballs and simmer for 10 minutes.

- Meanwhile, cook the rice noodles according to the pack instructions, then drain and serve with the meatballs and tomato sauce, garnished with the coriander leaves.

Thai Stir-Fry Chicken with

Noodles Cook 350 g (11½ oz) rice noodles in boiling water for 8–10 minutes, or according to the pack instructions. Meanwhile, toss 450 g (14½ oz) chicken breast strips with 2 tablespoons sesame oil, 1 deseeded and diced red chilli, 2 tablespoons peeled and grated fresh root ginger and 3 chopped spring onions. Heat 1 tablespoon vegetable oil in a wok, add the chicken and stir-fry for 3–4 minutes. Add 2 tablespoons red Thai curry paste and stir-fry for a further 2 minutes, then add 2 chopped pak choi and 300 ml (½ pint) coconut cream and bring to a boil. Simmer for 2–3 minutes. Drain the noodles and divide between 4 bowls. Spoon over the chicken.

Thai Chicken Curry with Noodles

Heat 1 tablespoon vegetable oil in a wok over a high heat, add 2 diced shallots and 1 diced stick of lemon grass and cook for 1–2 minutes. Stir in 3–4 teaspoons red Thai curry paste and cook for 1 minute, stirring. Add 600 g (1¼ lb) chicken breasts cut into bite-sized pieces and stir-fry for 5–6 minutes. Add ½ tablespoon fish sauce, 1 teaspoon brown sugar and a couple of kaffir lime leaves with a 400 ml (14 fl oz) can of coconut milk. Bring to a simmer and cook for 15 minutes. Cook 150 g (5 oz) rice noodles according to the pack instructions. Stir a small handful of roughly torn coriander leaves into the curry and serve with the rice noodles.

20 Seafood Stir-Fry

Serves 4

2 teaspoons clear honey
grated rind and juice of 1 lime
2 tablespoons tamari soy sauce
24 raw peeled tiger or jumbo king
  prawns
50 g (2 oz) squid rings
125 g (4 oz) mussels, shelled
150 g (5 oz) ribbon rice noodles
1 tablespoon vegetable oil
1 teaspoon sesame oil
4 spring onions, sliced
1 red pepper, deseeded and sliced
150 g (5 oz) bean sprouts
150 g (5 oz) pak choi, chopped

- Mix together the honey, lime rind and juice and the tamari. Place the prawns, squid and mussels in a bowl, pour over the marinade and leave for 5 minutes.

- Meanwhile, cook the noodles according to the pack instructions.

- Heat the oils in a wok over a high heat, add the drained seafood and stir-fry for 2–3 minutes, until the prawns have turned pink. Remove and set aside.

- Add the spring onions and red pepper and stir-fry for 2 minutes, then add the bean sprouts and pak choi and stir-fry for a further 1–2 minutes. Return the seafood to the pan with the drained rice noodles and stir-fry for 2–3 minutes. Serve immediately.

10 Seafood Salad

Heat 1 tablespoon olive oil in a frying pan over a medium heat, add 1 crushed garlic clove, ½ deseeded and diced red chilli and 500 g (1 lb) mixed seafood and cook for 4–5 minutes. Remove from the heat and remove the seafood from the pan with a slotted spoon. Stir 3 tablespoons lime juice and 2 tablespoons extra virgin olive oil into the pan. Toss the seafood with 100 g (3½ oz) rocket leaves and the dressing to serve.

30 Seafood Soup

Heat 1 tablespoon olive oil in a pan over a medium heat, add 4 sliced spring onions, 1 sliced celery stick, 1 deseeded and diced red chilli and 2 sliced garlic cloves and cook for 3–4 minutes. Pour in a 400 g (13 oz) can of chopped tomatoes and 600 ml (1 pint) fish stock and bring to a simmer, then cook for 10–12 minutes. Stir in 500 g (1 lb) mixed seafood or fish and cook for 4–5 minutes. Serve sprinkled with 2 tablespoons chopped parsley and with toasted gluten-free bread on the side.

 # Sausage and Onion Roast with Mustard Mash

Serves 4

8 gluten-free sausages

4 red onions, cut into wedges

2 leeks, thickly sliced

3–4 rosemary sprigs

2 tablespoons olive oil

875 g (1¾ lb) potatoes, peeled and cut into chunks

50 g (2 oz) butter

2–3 tablespoons wholegrain mustard

pepper

- Place the sausages, onions and leeks in a large roasting tin, toss with the rosemary and oil and season with pepper. Roast in a preheated oven, 200°C (400°F), Gas Mark 6, for 25 minutes, tossing a couple of times during the cooking time.

- Meanwhile, cook the potatoes in a pan of boiling water for 12–15 minutes, until tender.

- Drain the potatoes, return to the pan and mash with the butter until smooth. Stir in the wholegrain mustard.

- Divide the mustard mash between 4 warmed shallow bowls. Spoon over the sausages, roast vegetables and any juices from the roasting tin.

 ### Quick Sausage, Onion and Mash

Heat 1 tablespoon olive oil in a large frying pan, add 8 gluten-free sausages and cook for 10 minutes, turning regularly, until cooked through. Meanwhile, in a separate pan, heat 1 tablespoon olive oil, add 4 sliced red onions and cook for 2–3 minutes, then stir in 2 teaspoons balsamic vinegar and 1 teaspoon caster sugar and cook for a further 5–6 minutes. Meanwhile, cook 500 g (1 lb) ready-made mashed potato in a microwave according to the pack instructions, then stir in 2 tablespoons wholegrain mustard. Serve the sausages and onions with the mustard mash.

 ### Sausage and Onion Kebabs with Lemon Mash

Cook 675 g (1 lb 5 oz) potatoes, peeled and cut into chunks, in a pan of boiling water for 12–15 minutes until tender. Meanwhile, thread 8 chopped gluten-free sausages, 2 onions, cut into wedges, 2 deseeded and chopped red peppers and 1 deseeded and chopped yellow pepper onto 8 skewers, presoaked in cold water to prevent burning. Brush with 2 tablespoons olive oil and sprinkle with 2 tablespoons chopped rosemary. Place under a preheated hot grill and grill for 10–12 minutes, turning regularly. Drain the potatoes and mash with 50 g (2 oz) butter, the grated rind of 1 lemon and 1 tablespoon crème fraîche. Serve the kebabs with the lemon mash and a few sprigs of watercress.

10 Cheat's Pancetta and Broccoli Pizza

Serves 4

12 slices pancetta

4 gluten-free pitta breads

200 g (7 oz) Tenderstem broccoli, trimmed and cut into bite-sized pieces

200 g (7 oz) grated mozzarella cheese

- Place the pancetta under a hot grill and cook for 4–5 minutes, until crisp.

- Meanwhile, toast the pitta breads for 1–2 minutes on each side. Cook the broccoli in a pan of boiling water for 2 minutes, then drain.

- Place 2 slices of the pancetta on each pitta bread and divide the broccoli between them. Sprinkle with the mozzarella and place under the hot grill for 2–3 minutes, until golden and bubbling.

2 Fusilli with Purple Sprouting Broccoli and Pancetta

Cook 200 g (7 oz) pancetta, cut into strips, in a frying pan for 8–10 minutes, then add 4 sliced garlic cloves and fry for a further 1 minute. Pour in 4 tablespoons white wine and simmer for 4–5 minutes. Meanwhile, cook 350 g (11½ oz) gluten-free fusilli in a pan of boiling water for 9–12 minutes, or according to the pack instructions, adding 250 g (8 oz) trimmed and chopped purple sprouting broccoli 2 minutes before the end of the cooking time. Drain the pasta and broccoli, then toss with the pancetta and 100 g (3½ oz) grated Parmesan to serve.

3 Purple Sprouting Broccoli, Chilli and Pancetta Pizza

Cook 250 g (8 oz) trimmed and halved purple sprouting broccoli in boiling water for 2–3 minutes. Drain. Spread 2 large gluten-free pizza bases with 175 g (6 oz) ready-made pizza sauce. Add the broccoli and sprinkle over 200 g (7 oz) diced pancetta and 1 teaspoon dried chilli flakes. Top with ½ red onion, sliced, and 250 g (8 oz) sliced mozzarella. Bake in a preheated oven, 220°C (425°F), Gas Mark 7, for 22–25 minutes, until golden and bubbling.

Grilled Calves' Liver with Sage Lentils

Serves 4

1 tablespoon olive oil

1 carrot, peeled and diced

1 celery stick, diced

½ small red onion, finely diced

4 sage leaves, roughly torn

1 garlic clove, sliced

400 g (13 oz) can Puy lentils,
  rinsed and drained

125 ml (4 fl oz) red wine

100 g (3½ oz) baby spinach
  leaves

2–3 tablespoons crème fraîche

4 unsmoked streaky bacon
  rashers

400 g (13 oz) calves' liver

salt and pepper

- Heat the oil in a frying pan over a medium heat, add the carrot, celery and onion and cook for 2–3 minutes, then stir in the sage, garlic and lentils. Pour in the wine, add the spinach and crème fraîche and cook for 8–10 minutes.

- Meanwhile, cook the bacon under a preheated medium grill for 7 minutes or until crisp, then chop roughly.

- Season the liver with salt and pepper. Place under a hot grill or on a hot griddle and cook for 1–2 minutes on each side.

- Serve the liver on a bed of lentils, sprinkled with the chopped bacon.

Liver with Onions and Sage Mash

Heat 1 tablespoon olive oil in a frying pan, add 3 sliced onions and cook for 6–7 minutes. Add a dash of balsamic vinegar and ½ teaspoon sugar and cook for a further 2–3 minutes. In another pan, fry 450 g (14½ oz) sliced lambs' liver in 25 g (1 oz) butter for 1–2 minutes on each side. Meanwhile, heat 500 g (1 lb) ready-made mashed potato in a microwave according to the pack instructions and stir in 1 tablespoon chopped sage. Divide the mash between 4 plates, top with the liver and caramelized onions and serve immediately.

Cheese and Sage Chicken Livers with Lentil Salad

Heat 1 tablespoon olive oil in a saucepan, add 1 diced carrot, 1 diced celery stick, 1 small diced red onion and 2 sliced garlic cloves and cook for 2–3 minutes. Add a 400 g (13 oz) can of lentils, rinsed and drained, and cook for a further 2–3 minutes, then remove from the heat. Whisk together 3 tablespoons olive oil, 1 tablespoon red wine vinegar, ½ teaspoon Dijon mustard and ½ teaspoon clear honey. In a shallow bowl, mix together 100 g (3½ oz) polenta, 100 g (3½ oz) grated Parmesan, ½ tablespoon chopped sage and ½ teaspoon pepper. Beat 2 eggs and place in another shallow bowl. Melt 25 g (1 oz) butter with 1 tablespoon olive oil in a frying pan. Dip 500 g (1 lb) chicken livers first into the egg and then the polenta mixture, then add to the pan and fry for 2–3 minutes on each side. Drain on kitchen paper. Toss the lentils with 175 g (6 oz) mixed salad leaves and the dressing, and top with the liver.

30 Chicken en Papillote with Celeriac Mash

Serves 4

800 g (1 lb 4 oz) potatoes, peeled and cut into chunks

200 g (7 oz) celeriac, peeled and cut into chunks

4 x 150 g (5 oz) chicken breasts

8 tarragon sprigs

125 ml (4 fl oz) white wine

250 g (8 oz) green beans, trimmed

50 g (2 oz) butter

salt and pepper

- Cook the potatoes and celeriac together in a pan of boiling water for 10–12 minutes, until tender.

- Meanwhile, place each chicken breast on a large piece of greaseproof paper. Place 2 tarragon sprigs on each, then sprinkle with 2 tablespoons white wine and pepper. Fold the paper to securely enclose the chicken and liquid and place the parcels on a baking sheet or in a roasting tin.

- Bake in a preheated oven, 200°C (400°F), Gas Mark 6, for 15–18 minutes.

- Meanwhile, steam the beans for 3–4 minutes.

- Drain the potato and celeriac and mash together with the butter. Season with salt and pepper.

- Serve the chicken on a bed of mash, topped with the beans. Pour over any cooking juices.

 ### Griddled Chicken with Mash

Flatten 4 x 150 g (5 oz) chicken breasts with a rolling pin. Mix together 4 tablespoons lemon juice, 2 tablespoons honey and 1 tablespoon chopped tarragon and toss the chicken in the mixture. Cook on a hot griddle for 4 minutes on each side, until cooked through. Meanwhile, boil 250 g (8 oz) green beans for 3–4 minutes and heat 500 g (1 lb) ready-made mashed potato in a microwave according to the pack instructions. Stir 25 g (1 oz) butter through the potato and serve with the chicken and beans.

 ### Mash-Topped Chicken Pie

Heat 1 tablespoon olive oil in a saucepan over a medium heat, add 4 x 150 g (5 oz) chopped chicken breasts and 1 sliced onion and cook for 4–5 minutes. Add 150 ml (¼ pint) chicken stock and cook for a further 12–14 minutes. Meanwhile, heat 750 g (1½ lb) ready-made mashed potato in the microwave according to the pack instructions. Stir a 325 g (11 oz) can sweetcorn, drained, into the chicken mixture with 2 tablespoons crème fraîche, ½ tablespoon chopped tarragon and 1 tablespoon chopped parsley. Season with salt and pepper and spoon into 4 pie dishes. Top with the mashed potato and serve.

Stir-Fried Mixed Vegetables with Cashew Nuts

Serves 4

2 tablespoons groundnut oil

50 g (2 oz) cashew nuts

2 cm (¾ inch) piece of fresh root ginger, peeled and finely chopped

250 g (8 oz) Chinese leaves or cabbage, shredded

50 g (2 oz) cauliflower florets

60 g (2½ oz) broccoli florets

1 red pepper, deseeded and sliced

6 baby corn, halved lengthways

4 garlic cloves, chopped

1 tablespoon tamari soy sauce

- Heat the oil in a wok over a high heat, add the cashew nuts and ginger and stir-fry for 1 minute.

- Mix together the remaining ingredients in a bowl, then throw into the wok and cook over a high heat for 4–5 minutes, stirring and turning continuously. Serve immediately.

 Cashew Nut Pâté with Vegetable Crudités Heat ½ tablespoon olive oil in a frying pan over a high heat, add 150 g (5 oz) diced chestnut mushrooms and cook for 3–4 minutes. Add 175 g (6 oz) cashew nuts and cook for a further 3–4 minutes. Transfer into a food processor with 2 sliced spring onions, 1 tablespoon tahini paste, 2 tablespoons olive oil, 1 tablespoon natural yogurt and salt and pepper. Blend until nearly smooth. Adjust the seasoning, if necessary, and serve with vegetable crudités.

 Vegetable and Cashew Curry Toast 75 g (3 oz) cashew nuts in a dry frying pan over a medium heat for 2–3 minutes, then tip into a bowl and set aside. Heat 1 tablespoon sunflower oil in the frying pan, add 1 chopped onion and cook for 2–3 minutes. Add 1 deseeded and chopped red pepper, 125 g (4 oz) mangetout, 60 g (2½ oz) broccoli florets and 125 g (4 oz) baby corn and cook, stirring, for 2–3 minutes. Stir in 1 tablespoon Thai curry paste and a 400 ml (14 fl oz) can of coconut milk and simmer for 12–15 minutes, until the vegetables are tender. Stir in half of the toasted cashew nuts. Serve on warmed plates, scattered with the remaining nuts.

QuickCook

Sweet
Things
and Baking

Recipes listed by cooking time

30

20

10

30 Sweet Orange Pancakes

Serves 4

200 g (7 oz) plain gluten-free flour

2 eggs

300 ml (½ pint) milk

½ tablespoon sunflower oil, for oiling

2 oranges

2–3 tablespoons caster sugar, to serve

- Sift the flour into a bowl and make a well in the centre.

- Add the eggs and whisk, using a hand-held electric whisk, while gradually adding the milk and bringing the flour into the batter. Leave to stand for 10 minutes.

- Heat a small frying pan over a medium heat. Lightly oil the pan by wiping it with an oiled piece of kitchen paper.

- Pour a generous tablespoon of the batter into the pan and roll it around to completely coat the base of the pan. Cook for 3–4 minutes then turn over and cook the other side for 2–3 minutes.

- Place on a piece of baking paper and keep warm. Repeat with the remaining batter to make 8 pancakes.

- Grate the orange rind, then segment the oranges, catching the juice. Pour the juice into another pan, add the segments and rind and warm through. Pour over the pancakes to serve, with a sprinkling of sugar.

 ### Sweet Orange Drop Scones

Whisk together 200 g (7 oz) self-raising gluten-free flour, 2 eggs, 2 teaspoons sugar and 300 ml (½ pint) milk. Heat a little sunflower oil in a frying pan. Add spoonfuls of the batter to the pan and cook for 1–2 minutes. When air bubbles start to show on the surface, flip the scones over and cook for a further 1–2 minutes on the other side. Stir the grated rind of 2 oranges through 200 g (7 oz) natural yogurt and serve with the scones.

 ### Sweet Orange Scones

Sift together 250 g (8 oz) self-raising gluten-free flour and 1 teaspoon gluten-free baking powder. Rub in 50 g (2 oz) butter until the mixture resembles fine breadcrumbs, then stir in 50 g (2 oz) caster sugar and the grated rind of 1 orange. Lightly beat together 1 egg and 125 ml (4 fl oz) milk and stir into the flour mixture to make a soft dough. Turn out onto a lightly floured work surface and lightly press until about 2 cm (¾ inch) thick. Using a 3–4 cm (1½ inch) cutter, cut into 8–10 rounds and place on a baking sheet. Bake in a preheated oven, 200°C (400°F), Gas Mark 6, for 15–16 minutes until risen and lightly browned. Serve warm spread with butter or a dollop of cream.

10 Petit Pots au Chocolat

Serves 4

175 g (6 oz) plain dark chocolate,
roughly chopped
1 tablespoon brandy
200 ml (7 fl oz) double cream
4 tablespoons crème fraîche
cocoa powder, for dusting

- Place the chocolate in a heatproof bowl set over a saucepan of gently simmering water and stir until melted.

- Warm the brandy and cream in a small saucepan over a medium heat until hot but not boiling. Stir into the chocolate until completely blended.

- Spoon the chocolate mixture into 4 cups or ramekins and chill until firm.

- Serve topped with a dollop of crème fraîche and dusted with cocoa powder.

2 Chocolate Puddings

In a heatproof bowl set over a saucepan of gently simmering water, melt together 185 g (6½ oz) chocolate and 150 g (5 oz) butter, stirring occasionally until smooth. In another bowl, whisk together 2 eggs and 2 egg yolks with 2 tablespoons caster sugar. Whisk in the chocolate mixture, then sift in 2 teaspoons self-raising gluten-free flour and fold it in. Divide the mixture between 4 pudding moulds or ramekin dishes and bake in a preheated oven, 200°C (400°F), Gas Mark 6, for 9–10 minutes until cooked on the outside but still soft inside.
Serve warm.

3 Chocolate Muffins

In a large bowl, mix together 200 g (7 oz) self-raising gluten-free flour, 4 tablespoons cocoa powder and 200 g (7 oz) caster sugar. Rub in 125 g (4 oz) unsalted butter until the mixture resembles fine breadcrumbs. Whisk together 2 eggs and 125 ml (4 fl oz) milk, then stir into the flour mixture. Line a 12-hole muffin tin with paper cases, spoon in the mixture and bake in a preheated oven, 200°C (400°F), Gas Mark 6, for 20 minutes until risen.

Coconut and Raspberry Muffins

Serves 4

225 g (7½ oz) self-raising gluten-free flour

1 teaspoon gluten-free baking powder

½ teaspoon bicarbonate of soda

75 g (3 oz) caster sugar

40 g (1¾ oz) desiccated coconut

55 g (2 oz) unsalted butter, melted

2 eggs

150 ml (¼ pint) milk

125 g (4 oz) raspberries

- Line a 12-hole muffin tin with paper muffin cases.

- In a large bowl, sift together the flour, baking powder and bicarbonate of soda, then mix in the sugar and coconut. Make a well in the centre.

- Whisk together the melted butter, eggs and milk.

- Add the wet ingredients to the dry and mix together gently, adding the raspberries when nearly combined – do not over mix.

- Spoon into the paper cases. Bake in a preheated oven, 200°C (400°F), Gas Mark 6, for 15 minutes until golden and slightly risen.

- Cool on a wire rack.

 Coconut and Raspberry Yogurt Pudding Toast 4 tablespoons desiccated coconut under a preheated medium grill for 3–4 minutes, until lightly golden. Stir into 500 ml (17 fl oz) natural yogurt with 125 g (4 oz) raspberries. Divide between 4 small bowls or glasses and serve sprinkled with a few raspberries on top and a drizzle of honey.

 Coconut Scones with Raspberries Sift 250 g (8 oz) self-raising gluten-free flour into a bowl with 1 teaspoon gluten-free baking powder. Stir in 1 tablespoon desiccated coconut. Rub in 50 g (2 oz) unsalted butter until the mixture resembles fine breadcrumbs. Stir in 50 g (2 oz) caster sugar. Whisk together 1 egg and 150 ml (¼ pint) milk and pour this into the flour mixture. Bring the dough together. Using an ice cream scoop, scoop 8 mounds of the dough onto a baking sheet. Bake in a preheated oven, 220°C (425°F), Gas Mark 7, for 12–15 minutes until risen and golden. Serve warm with dollops of clotted cream and some fresh raspberries.

10 Caramelized Pears with Salted Caramel Sauce

Serves 4

100 g (3½ oz) unsalted butter
100 g (3½ oz) soft light brown sugar
50 g (2 oz) caster sugar
50 g (2 oz) golden syrup
125 ml (4 fl oz) double cream
1 teaspoon salt flakes
4 pears, peeled, halved and cored

- To make the salted caramel sauce, put 75 g (3 oz) of the butter, 75 g (3 oz) of the soft light brown sugar, the caster sugar and golden syrup in a small heavy-based saucepan. Place over a low heat to melt, stirring until the sugar has dissolved, then simmer for 3 minutes, stirring occasionally.

- Stir in the cream and half the salt. Carefully taste the caramel sauce, then add more salt if wished. Pour into a jug to cool a little.

- Meanwhile, melt the remaining butter and sugar in a frying pan, add the pears and cook for 4–5 minutes, until golden.

- Serve with the salted caramel sauce.

---

20 Apple and Pear Fritters with Salted Caramel Sauce

Place 140 g (4¾ oz) plain gluten-free flour in a bowl and whisk in 2 eggs, 2 egg yolks and 200 ml (7 fl oz) milk. Whisk 2 egg whites until they just start to hold their shape, then fold into the batter. Peel, halve and core 2 pears and 2 dessert apples, then cut into wedges. Put 1 tablespoon vegetable oil in a heavy-based saucepan over a medium heat and heat until a small piece of bread dropped into the oil sizzles and turns golden within 20 seconds. In 3–4 batches, dip the fruit into the batter, then carefully fry in the oil for 3–4 minutes until golden and crisp. Remove using a slotted spoon, drain on kitchen paper and toss with 1 teaspoon ground cinnamon and 75 g (3 oz) caster sugar. Serve with some Salted Caramel Sauce, made as above.

30 Pear Muffins with Salted Caramel

Sift together 225 g (7½ oz) self-raising gluten-free flour, 1 teaspoon gluten-free baking powder and ½ teaspoon bicarbonate of soda. Stir in 75 g (3 oz) sugar and make a well in the centre. Whisk together 55 g (2 oz) melted butter, 2 eggs and 150 ml (¼ pint) milk. Pour the wet ingredients into the dry and mix gently, then stir in 2 peeled, cored and diced pears. Line a 12-hole muffin tin with paper cases and spoon in the mixture. Bake in a preheated oven, 200°C (400°F), Gas Mark 6, for 15 minutes until risen and golden. Meanwhile, make the Salted Caramel Sauce as above. Serve the muffins warm with the sauce.

20 Rhubarb Fool

Serves 4

450 g (14½ oz) rhubarb, chopped into bite-sized pieces
2 tablespoons caster sugar
4 tablespoons white wine
300 ml (½ pint) double cream
finely grated rind of 1 lemon
1 egg white
chopped pistachios nuts, to serve

- Place the rhubarb and sugar into a saucepan over a low heat, pour in the wine and simmer over a low heat until cooked. Pour into a bowl and leave to cool.

- Whisk the cream until thick and stir into the rhubarb with the grated lemon rind.

- Whisk the egg white until stiff, then gently fold into the rhubarb mixture.

- Divide between 4 bowls and top with the chopped pistachios. Chill until required.

10 Quick Rhubarb Fool

Drain a 530 g (1 lb 2 oz) can of rhubarb and blend the rhubarb in a food processor to make a purée. Whisk 300 ml (½ pint) double cream with the grated rind of 1 lemon, then fold in the rhubarb purée. Taste for sweetness, adding a little honey to taste. Divide between 4 glasses and serve.

30 Roasted Rhubarb

Cut 550 g (1 lb 2 oz) rhubarb into finger-sized pieces. Place in a shallow ovenproof dish and toss with 85 g (3¼ oz) caster sugar, making sure the rhubarb is in a single layer. Cover with foil and roast in a preheated oven, 200°C (400°F), Gas Mark 6, for 15 minutes. Remove the foil and continue to cook for a further 5–6 minutes, until the rhubarb is tender and the juices are syrupy. Serve with vanilla ice cream.

30 Tropical Salsa with Ice Cream

Serves 4

1 passion fruit

1 ripe mango, stoned, peeled and finely diced

100 g (3½ oz) pineapple, finely diced

1 piece of preserved stem ginger, finely diced

1 teaspoon preserved stem ginger syrup

1 teaspoon finely shredded mint

½ teaspoon finely shredded coriander leaves

ice cream of your choice, to serve

- Halve the passion fruit and scoop the pulp into a sieve over a bowl and press the seeds to get all the juice out. Discard the seeds.

- Add the finely diced fruit and ginger to the bowl, then stir in the ginger syrup.

- Finally, stir in the shredded herbs. Leave to stand at room temperature for 20 minutes to allow the flavours to infuse.

- When ready to serve, spoon over your favourite ice cream for an instant tropical dessert.

10 Tropical Eton Mess

Place 40 g (1¾ oz) broken meringue in a large bowl and add 100 g (3½ oz) diced pineapple, 1 peeled, stoned and diced mango and 300 g (10 oz) natural yogurt. Stir in 1 diced piece of preserved stem ginger and ½ tablespoon chopped mint. Mix very gently so you do not break up the meringue pieces too much. Divide between 4 small glasses or bowls to serve.

20 Tropical Winter Fruit Salad

Place 10 peeled and stoned lychees in a large bowl with 1 small pineapple, peeled and cut into chunks, 1 peeled and stoned mango, cut into chunks, the seeds of 1 pomegranate and 6 diced medjool dates. Scrape the pulp from 3 passion fruit and sieve to remove the pips. Gently stir the passion fruit juice through the salad and check to see if any sweetness is required – if so, add a little honey. Leave to sit at room temperature for a few minutes, then serve with dollops of crème fraîche sprinkled with ground nutmeg.

Baked Apples with Spiced Fruit

Serves 4

4 cooking apples, cored and
  scored around the middle
75 g (3 oz) dried cranberries
4 pieces of preserved stem
  ginger, diced
finely grated rind of 2 oranges
½ teaspoon mixed spice
4 tablespoons clear honey
crème fraîche, to serve

- Place the apples in an ovenproof dish. Mix together the cranberries, ginger, orange rind, mixed spice and honey and spoon the mixture into the cavity of each apple.

- Pour 2 tablespoons water into the dish. Bake in a preheated oven, 190°C (375°F), Gas Mark 5, for 22–25 minutes until the apples are puffy and cooked through. Serve with crème fraîche.

 **Spiced Apples**

Melt 25 g (1 oz) butter in a frying pan over a medium heat, add 4 peeled, cored and sliced apples and ½ tablespoon mixed spice and cook for 5–6 minutes. Stir in 2 tablespoons honey and serve with crème fraîche.

 Spiced Apple Scones

Sift 250 g (8 oz) self-raising gluten-free flour into a bowl with 1 teaspoon gluten-free baking powder and ½ teaspoon ground cinnamon. Rub in 50 g (2 oz) unsalted butter until the mixture resembles fine breadcrumbs. Stir in 50 g (2 oz) caster sugar. Whisk together 1 egg and 150 ml (¼ pint) milk and pour into the flour mixture. Bring the dough together. Using an ice cream scoop, scoop 8 mounds of dough onto a baking sheet. Bake in a preheated oven, 220°C (425°F), Gas Mark 7, for 12–15 minutes until risen and golden. Meanwhile, melt 25 g (1 oz) butter in a saucepan, add 2 cored and sliced dessert apples and cook for 3–4 minutes. Take off the heat and sprinkle with 2 teaspoons caster sugar and ¼ teaspoon ground cinnamon. Serve the scones split in half and topped with a little apple and a dollop of crème fraîche.

1 Blueberry and Date Mousse

Serves 4

75 g (3 oz) dates
75 g (3 oz) pitted prunes
grated rind of 1 orange
2 tablespoons crème fraîche
3–4 tablespoons natural yogurt
100 g (3½ oz) blueberries
grated plain dark chocolate, to
serve

- Place the dates and prunes in a food processor with the orange rind and process until broken down.

- Add the crème fraîche, the yogurt and the blueberries and process again until you have a mousse-like texture.

- Spoon into 4 glasses and sprinkle with a little grated chocolate to serve.

2 Blueberry and Date Flapjacks

In a heavy-based saucepan, melt together 100 g (3½ oz) coconut oil, 90 g (3¼ oz) blackstrap molasses, 20 g (¾ oz) dark muscovado sugar and 25 g (1 oz) agave syrup until the sugar has dissolved. Stir in 250 g (8 oz) rolled oats, 50 g (2 oz) dried blueberries and 50 g (2 oz) chopped dates. Spoon into a lightly greased 18 cm (7 inch) tin and bake in a preheated oven, 180°C (350°F), Gas Mark 4, for 15–16 minutes. Leave to cool for 2 minutes, then cut into squares and leave to cool completely in the tin.

3 Blueberry and Date Muffins

Sift together 225 g (7½ oz) self-raising gluten-free flour with 1 tablespoon gluten-free baking powder and ½ teaspoon bicarbonate of soda. Stir in 75 g (3 oz) sugar and make a well in the centre. Whisk together 50 g (2 oz) melted unsalted butter, 2 eggs and 150 ml (¼ pint) milk. Add the wet ingredients to the dry and mix together gently, adding 125 g (4 oz) blueberries when nearly mixed – do not over mix. Line a 12-hole muffin tin with paper cases, spoon in the mixture and bake in a preheated oven, 200°C (400°F)

Gas Mark 6, for 15 minutes until risen and golden. Remove from the tin and cool on a wire rack or serve warm.

 # Amaretti-Stuffed Peaches

Serves 4

4 ripe peaches, halved and stoned
8 amaretti biscuits, crushed
4 tablespoons mascarpone cheese
grated rind and juice of 1 orange

- Place the peaches in a shallow ovenproof dish, cut side up.

- Mix together the crushed biscuits, mascarpone and orange rind and divide the mixture into the halved peaches.

- Sprinkle with the orange juice and bake in a preheated oven, 200°C (400°F), Gas Mark 6, for 15–20 minutes, until tender.

 Quick Peach Amaretti Pudding

Mix together 200 g (7 oz) Greek yogurt with 200 g (7 oz) mascarpone cheese. Stir in the grated rind of 1 orange and 6 crushed amaretti biscuits. Stone and slice 4 peaches, divide between 4 plates, and serve each one with a generous dollop of the amaretti cream.

 Amaretti and Peach Trifle

Place 200 g (7 oz) amaretti biscuits in a glass bowl. Top with 6 stoned and chopped peaches and pour over 100 ml (3½ fl oz) Amaretto liqueur. Pour over 400 ml (14 fl oz) ready-made custard to cover. Whisk 300 ml (½ pint) double cream to soft peaks and spoon over the trifle. Sprinkle with 50 g (2 oz) toasted flaked almonds. Chill for 10 minutes before serving.

30 Florentines

Serves 4

50 g (2 oz) unsalted butter
100 g (3½ oz) golden caster sugar
50 ml (2 fl oz) thick double cream
175 g (6 oz) flaked almonds
25 g (1 oz) chopped mixed peel
1 egg white
100 g (3½ oz) plain dark
  chocolate, melted

- Line 2 baking sheets with baking paper.

- Place the butter and sugar in a small saucepan with 50 ml (2 fl oz) water. Bring to the boil, then cook on a high heat for 5 minutes until the mixture starts to turn pale. Remove from the heat and leave to cook for 2 minutes.

- Stir in the cream, almonds and mixed peel.

- Whisk the egg white to soft peaks, then gently fold into the almond mixture.

- Spoon the mixture onto the prepared baking sheets to make 12 Florentines, leaving space between each one.

- Bake in a preheated oven, 180 °C (350 °F), Gas Mark 4, for 15–18 minutes, until golden. Carefully slide onto a wire rack and leave to cool.

- Spread the bottom of each Florentine with melted dark chocolate and leave to set.

 Almond and Mixed Peel Muesli

Mix together 200 g (7 oz) rolled oats, 150 g (5 oz) mixed dried fruits (including chopped mixed peel) and 100 g (3½ oz) flaked almonds. Serve with milk, natural yogurt and fresh fruit.

 Orange and Almond Muffins

Mix together 225 g (7½ oz) gluten-free self-raising flour, 1 tablespoon gluten-free baking powder, 75 g (3 oz) caster sugar, ½ teaspoon bicarbonate of soda, 50 g (2 oz) diced mixed peel, grated rind of 1 orange and 50 g (2 oz) flaked almonds. Whisk together 55 g (2 oz) melted butter, 2 eggs and 150 ml (¼ pint) milk and pour into the dry ingredients. Line a 12-hole muffin tin with paper cases, spoon in the mixture and bake in a preheated oven, 200 °C (400 °F), Gas Mark 6, for 15 minutes until golden.

 # Spicy Griddled Pineapple

Serves 4

8 slices of fresh pineapple, peeled and cored
1 tablespoon clear honey
pinch of dried chilli flakes
pinch of ground cinnamon
crème fraîche or natural yogurt, to serve

- Heat a frying pan or griddle pan until very hot. Add the pineapple slices and cook until they start to caramelize. Turn them over just once.

- Add the honey, chilli flakes and cinnamon and cook until the mixture starts to bubble – this will not take long.

- Serve the pineapple slices drizzled with the spicy honey and a dollop of crème fraîche or natural yogurt.

 Spicy Pineapple Smoothie

Roughly chop 1 small peeled pineapple and 1 banana and place in a blender with 2 teaspoons honey, a pinch of dried chilli flakes and a pinch of cinnamon. Pour in 400 ml (14 fl oz) milk and 2–3 tablespoons natural yogurt and blend until smooth, adding more milk if needed, to give a thick creamy smoothie.

Pineapple Fritters Make the batter by putting 125 g (4 oz) plain gluten-free flour into a bowl with 45 g (2 oz) caster sugar and a pinch of salt. Add 1 egg, 1 egg yolk and 150 ml (¼ pint) milk and whisk to make a smooth batter. In another clean bowl, whisk 1 egg white until it forms stiff peaks and gently fold into the batter. Leave the batter to stand for 10 minutes. Heat 500 ml (17 fl oz) sunflower oil in a saucepan until a small cube of bread sizzles and browns when dropped into the oil. Peel, core and slice 1 pineapple into rings. Dip the pineapple rings into the batter and cook in the oil in batches for 3–4 minutes, until golden on both sides. Remove from the pan and drain on kitchen paper. Sprinkle with icing sugar. Serve with a dollop of natural yogurt or crème fraîche, with a sprinkling of grated nutmeg or ground cinnamon.

30 Sticky Rice and Mango

Serves 4

250 g (8 oz) long grain rice
200 ml (7 fl oz) coconut milk
60 g (2½ oz) caster sugar
4–5 cardamom pods, bruised
2 mangoes, stoned, peeled and
  sliced

- Wash the rice in a few changes of water, then leave to soak for 10 minutes.

- Drain the rice and place in a saucepan with 300 ml (½ pint) water. Bring to the boil and leave to boil for 1 minute. Reduce the heat, cover and leave to simmer for 8–9 minutes, until all the water has been absorbed.

- Meanwhile, mix together the coconut milk and sugar. Add the bruised cardamom pods.

- Pour the coconut mixture into the rice and slowly bring to the boil, then simmer for 10 minutes, stirring occasionally – do not let it stick. Turn off the heat and leave to stand for 5 minutes.

- Serve the sticky rice with slices of fresh mango.

 1 Quick Cardamom Rice Pudding with Mango In a saucepan, heat the crushed seeds of 4–5 cardamom pods with 2–3 tablespoons double cream to infuse the cream with the cardamom flavour. Stir in a 400 g (13 oz) can of rice pudding and heat according to the pack instructions. Meanwhile, heat 1 tablespoon clear honey in a frying pan, add 2 stoned, peeled and sliced mangoes and cook for 3–4 minutes, until starting to caramelize. Serve the mango with the cardamom rice pudding.

 2 Mango and Cardamom Muffins Sift together 225 g (7½ oz) self-raising gluten-free flour with 1 teaspoon gluten-free baking powder and ½ teaspoon bicarbonate of soda. Stir in 75 g (3 oz) caster sugar and the crushed seeds of 4–5 cardamom pods. Whisk together 55 g (2 oz) melted unsalted butter, 2 eggs and 150 ml (¼ pint) milk. Pour the wet ingredients into the dry and mix gently, adding 1 stoned, peeled and diced mango when nearly mixed – do not over mix. Bake in a preheated oven, 200°C (400°F), Gas Mark 6, for 12–15 minutes until risen and golden.

GLU-SWEE-XAJ

 # Chilli Hot Chocolate

Serves 4

175 g (6 oz) plain dark chocolate, broken into pieces
1 large pinch of chilli powder
2 tablespoons caster sugar
2 large pinches of ground cinnamon
2 vanilla pods, split lengthways
600 ml (1 pt) milk
200 ml (7 fl oz) whipping cream, whipped
grated plain dark chocolate, to serve

- Place the chocolate, chilli powder, sugar, cinnamon, vanilla pods and milk into a pan and heat gently until the chocolate has melted.

- Bring to the boil and whisk until the chocolate is very smooth and frothy.

- Remove the vanilla pods.

- Pour the chocolate into 4 warmed mugs and top with the whipped cream and grated chocolate.

 ### Chilli Chocolate Mousse

Place 150 g (5 oz) plain dark chocolate and ¼ deseeded and finely diced red chilli into a food processor and process until chopped. Add 2 eggs and blend until nearly smooth. While the machine is running, pour in 150 ml (¼ pint) hot coffee and continue to blend until the mousse is completely smooth. Taste for sweetness and, if needed, add 1 teaspoon clear honey and blend again. Pour into 4 small glasses or bowls and place in the freezer for 15 minutes to set.

 ### Chilli Chocolate Cupcakes

Beat together 250 g (8 oz) softened butter, 250 g (8 oz) caster sugar and ¼ deseeded and finely diced red chilli until light and fluffy. Add 4 beaten eggs, one at a time, adding a little of 250 g (8 oz) self-raising gluten-free flour after each egg. Stir in the remaining flour and 3 tablespoons cocoa powder, then spoon the mixture into 12 paper cases in a 12-hole cupcake tin. Bake in a preheated oven, 190°C (375°F) Gas Mark 5, for 20 minutes. Remove from the tin, place on a wire rack and sprinkle with 100 g (3½ oz) grated plain dark chocolate and 25 g (1 oz) grated white chocolate.

20 Fruit-Stuffed Pancakes

Serves 4

115 g (3¾ oz) rice flour

1 teaspoon gluten-free baking powder

½ teaspoon ground cinnamon

1 egg

finely grated rind of 1 lemon

175 ml (6 fl oz) soya milk

2–3 teaspoons sunflower oil

1 peach, stoned and chopped

100 g (3½ oz) blueberries

60 g (2½ oz) raspberries

¼ cantaloupe melon, deseeded and chopped

5–6 mint leaves, shredded

4 tablespoons clear honey

natural yogurt, to serve

- Place the flour, baking powder, cinnamon, egg, lemon rind and milk in a food processor, add 2–3 tablespoons water and blend together.

- Heat half the oil in a frying pan over a medium heat, pour in one-quarter of the mixture and cook for 2–3 minutes, then flip the pancake over and cook for a further 1–2 minutes. Remove from the pan and keep warm. Repeat with the remaining batter, adding more oil to the pan if needed.

- Gently mix together the fruit. Spoon one-quarter of the fruit mixture into the middle of each pancake and sprinkle over some shredded mint. Fold the pancakes in half and place on a baking sheet. Drizzle over the honey and cook under a preheated hot grill for 2–3 minutes. Serve with a dollop of yogurt.

10 Fruit Smoothie

In a blender, blend together 1 chopped banana, 2 stoned and chopped peaches, ½ cantaloupe melon, deseeded and chopped, 100 g (3½ oz) raspberries, 200 g (7 oz) natural yogurt, 600 ml (1 pint) soya milk and 2–3 tablespoons clear honey. If liked, add a few ice cubes and blend again.

30 Roasted Mint Fruit Compote

Stone 3 peaches, 4 apricots and 4 plums and cut into wedges. Place in an ovenproof dish with 200 g (7 oz) blueberries and 200 g (7 oz) raspberries. Blitz 50 g (2 oz) caster sugar with 10–12 mint leaves, then toss the green sugar mixture into the fruit. Roast in a preheated oven, 190°C (375°F), Gas Mark 5, for 22–25 minutes. Serve with natural yogurt.

30 Blackberry and Apple Crumbles

Serves 4

4 dessert apples, peeled, cored
and thinly sliced
125 g (4 oz) blackberries
2 teaspoons caster sugar
100 g (3½ oz) rolled oats
50 g (2 oz) unsalted butter, diced
40 g (1¾ oz) dark muscovado
sugar
25 g (1 oz) flaked almonds

- Divide the apple slices and blackberries between 4 small ovenproof dishes or ramekins and sprinkle with the caster sugar.

- In a food processor, blitz the oats, butter, sugar and almonds. Spoon the oat mixture over the fruit and bake in a preheated oven, 190°C (375°F), Gas Mark 5, for 22–25 minutes until golden.

 Blackberry and Apple Fool

Whip 300 ml (½ pint) double cream until soft peaks form. Gently fold in 150 g (5 oz) puréed apple and 125 oz (4 oz) lightly crushed blackberries. Divide between 4 glasses and chill until ready to serve.

 Blackberry and Apple Muffins

Sift together 225 g (7½ oz) self-raising gluten-free flour, 1 tablespoon gluten-free baking powder and ½ teaspoon bicarbonate of soda. Stir in 75 g (3 oz) caster sugar and make a well in the centre. Whisk together 55 g (2 oz) melted unsalted butter, 2 eggs and 150 ml (¼ pint) milk. Add the wet ingredients to the dry and mix together gently, adding 100 g (3½ oz) blackberries and 1 peeled, cored and diced dessert apple when nearly combined – do not over mix. Divide between 12 paper muffin cases in a muffin tin and bake in a preheated oven, 200°C (400°F) Gas Mark 6, for 15 minutes until risen and golden. Cool on a wire rack or eat warm.

3 Date and Amaretti Tiramisu

Serves 4

6 dates, pitted and roughly
  chopped
100 ml (3½ fl oz) strong coffee
60 ml (2½ fl oz) Amaretto liqueur
2 eggs, separated
65 g (2 ½ oz) caster sugar
150 g (5 oz) mascarpone cheese
100 g (3½ oz) ricotta cheese
150 ml (¼ pint) whipping cream,
  whipped to soft peaks
125 g (4 oz) amaretti biscuits,
  lightly crushed
15 g (½ oz) cocoa powder

- Put the dates in a saucepan with the coffee and bring to the boil, then remove from the heat, stir in the Amaretto liqueur and leave to cool for 15 minutes.

- Whisk the egg whites and 2 tablespoons of the caster sugar to stiff peaks.

- In a separate bowl whisk the remaining sugar with the mascarpone, ricotta and egg yolks, then fold in the whipped cream. Finally, fold in the egg whites.

- Toss the amaretti biscuits with the dates, then spoon one-half of this mixture into 4 glasses. Sift over one-third of the cocoa powder.

- Top with one-half of the cream mixture, then repeat the layers with the remaining ingredients.

- Finish off with a sifting of cocoa powder. Chill until ready to serve.

1 Date and Coffee Dessert

In a small saucepan, bring 100 ml (3½ fl oz) strong coffee, 2 teaspoons caster sugar, 12 crushed cardamom pods and 1 cinnamon stick to the boil. Add 350 g (11½ oz) pitted dates, then remove from the heat and leave to stand for 8 minutes. Spoon the dates into 4 glasses, top with 400 g (13 oz) Greek yogurt and sift over 1 tablespoon cocoa powder to serve.

2 Individual Sticky Date and Coffee

Puddings Lightly grease a 12-hole muffin tin. Place 275 g (9 oz) pitted and chopped dates in a small saucepan with 250 ml (8 fl oz) weak coffee. Bring to the boil, then remove from the heat and stir in 1 teaspoon bicarbonate of soda. Add 60 g (2½ oz) unsalted butter and stir until it has melted. Sift 175 g (6 oz) plain gluten-free flour into a bowl, then stir in 125 g (4 oz) dark muscovado sugar. Make a well in the centre, pour in the date mixture and 2 beaten eggs

and mix together well. Spoon into the prepared muffin tin and cook in a preheated oven, 180°C (350°F), Gas Mark 5, for 15–18 minutes. Meanwhile, place 100 g (3½ oz) unsalted butter, 150 g (5 oz) light brown soft sugar, 2 tablespoons golden syrup and 185 ml (6½ fl oz) double cream in a saucepan over a low heat and cook, stirring, for 3–4 minutes. Bring to the boil and then simmer for 2 minutes. To serve, turn the puddings out onto serving plates, pour over the sauce and top with vanilla ice cream.

10 Eton Mess

Serves 4

500 g (1 lb) strawberries, hulled and chopped
1 teaspoon ginger cordial
400 ml (14 fl oz) double cream
3 ready-made meringue nests, lightly crushed
2 pieces of preserved stem ginger, diced
1 tablespoon shredded mint

- Toss the strawberries in a bowl with the ginger cordial.

- Whip the cream to soft peaks, then stir in the strawberries, crushed meringue, ginger and half the shredded mint.

- Divide between 4 glasses and sprinkle over the remaining shredded mint to serve.

2 Strawberry Cheesecakes

Melt 25 g (1 oz) unsalted butter in a small saucepan, then stir in 14 crushed amaretti biscuits. Spoon the biscuit mixture into 4 ramekins and press into the base. Chill for 5 minutes. Mix together 200 g (7 oz) Greek yogurt, 200 g (7 oz) cream cheese, 2 teaspoons caster sugar and 2 teaspoons chopped mint. Spoon the yogurt mixture over the biscuit base and level with a knife. Lightly crush 150 g (5 oz) hulled and diced strawberries and spoon over the cheesecakes to serve.

3 Mint-Marinated Strawberries

Place 200 g (7 oz) hulled and halved strawberries in a bowl with 50 g (2 oz) caster sugar and 2 tablespoons lemon juice. Lightly mash with a fork, then stir in another 200 g (7 oz) hulled and halved strawberries. Stir in 2 finely diced pieces of preserved stem ginger and 2 teaspoons finely chopped mint and leave to marinate in the fridge for 25 minutes. Serve spooned over clotted cream.

30 Chocolate Walnut Brownies

Serves 4

225 g (7½ oz) unsalted butter
225 g (7½ oz) plain dark
   chocolate, chopped
200 g (7 oz) golden caster sugar
3 eggs, beaten
150 g (5 oz) ground almonds
100 g (3½ oz) walnuts, chopped
vanilla ice cream, to serve

- Melt the butter and chocolate together in a small saucepan over a low heat. Stir in the sugar.

- Beat the eggs into the pan, then stir in the almonds and walnuts.

- Pour into a 23 cm (9 inch) square cake tin and bake in a preheated oven, 180°C (350°F), Gas Mark 4, for 25 minutes, until the top is set but the middle is still gooey.

- Serve warm with scoops of vanilla ice cream.

1 Quick Chocolate Walnut Mousse

Roughly chop 100 g (3½ oz) plain dark chocolate and put in a bowl. Pour 150 ml (¼ pint) double cream into a small saucepan and bring to the boil. Stir the hot cream into the chocolate to melt it, then pour in another 150 ml (¼ pint) cold double cream and 2 tablespoons Amaretto liqueur. Beat the chocolate mixture with a hand-held electric whisk until it forms soft peaks. In another grease-free bowl, whisk 1 large egg white and gradually add 50 g (2 oz) caster sugar, whisking until you have a soft meringue. Fold into the chocolate mixture, then spoon into glasses to serve. Serve sprinkled with 1 tablespoon toasted and chopped walnuts.

2 Chocolate Walnut Puddings

Melt together 150 g (5 oz) chopped plain dark chocolate and 150 g (5 oz) unsalted butter in a heatproof bowl set over a saucepan of gently simmering water. Remove from the heat, add 150 ml (¼ pint) warm water and 100 g (3½ oz) caster sugar and stir until smooth. Lightly beat 4 egg yolks and whisk into the chocolate mixture. Fold in 25 g (1 oz) sifted rice flour, 25 g (1 oz) toasted and finely chopped walnuts and 1 teaspoon gluten-free baking powder. Whisk 4 egg whites in a grease-free bowl until stiff, then gently fold into the chocolate mixture. Pour into 4 greased ramekins. Bake in a preheated oven, 200°C (400°F) Gas Mark 6, for 12–15 minutes until the top is firm and the middle still soft and fudgy. Serve with a dollop of crème fraîche, dusted with cocoa powder.

30 Lemon Yogurt Fairy Cakes

Makes 12

175 g (6 oz) plain gluten-free flour

½ teaspoon gluten-free baking powder

175 g (6 oz) caster sugar

150 g (5 oz) unsalted butter, melted

2 eggs

60 ml (2 fl oz) natural yogurt

grated rind of 2 lemons

For the icing

175 g (6 oz) unsalted butter, softened

400 g (13 oz) icing sugar, sifted

grated rind of 1 lemon, plus extra for sprinkling

- Line a 12-hole bun tin with paper cases.

- In a bowl sift together the flour and baking powder, then st in the sugar.

- Whisk together the melted butter, eggs, yogurt and lemon rind. Pour into the dry ingredients and mix lightly until combined.

- Divide the mixture between the paper cases. Bake in a preheated oven, 180°C (350°F), Gas Mark 4, for 15–18 minutes, until golden. Leave to cool on a wire rack.

- Beat together the softened butter, icing sugar and grated lemon rind.

- Pipe or spoon the icing on to the fairy cakes and sprinkle with extra grated lemon rind.

 Lemon Yogurt Pudding

Stir 3 tablespoons lemon curd and the grated rind of 1 lemon into 500 g (1 lb) Greek yogurt. Divide between 4 glasses, sprinkle with 4 teaspoons dark muscovado sugar and chill for 5 minutes.

 Lemon Puddings with Greek Yogurt

Spoon 1 teaspoon lemon curd into 4 ramekins. Place 125 g (4 oz) each of plain gluten-free flour, caster sugar and softened butter in a food processor, add 2 tablespoons gluten-free baking powder, 2 eggs and the grated rind of 1 lemon and process. Divide the mixture between th 4 ramekins. Bake in a preheate oven, 190°C (375°F), Gas Mar 5, for 16–18 minutes. Serve wi a dollop of Greek yogurt and grated lemon rind.

20 Banoffee Pie

Serves 4

200 g (7 oz) amaretti biscuits, lightly crushed

100 g (3½ oz) unsalted butter, melted

397 g (13 oz) can caramel

3 bananas, sliced

200 ml (7 fl oz) double cream

30 g (1¼ oz) plain dark chocolate, grated

- Place the crushed amaretti biscuits in a bowl, pour over the melted butter and mix well.

- Pour the buttered crumbs into a 20 cm (8 inch) loose-bottomed flan tin and press then into the base and sides. Chill for 10 minutes.

- Spread the caramel over the biscuit base, then top with the sliced bananas.

- Whip the cream to soft peaks and spread over the bananas.

- Scatter the grated chocolate over the top.

 Banana Toffee Dessert

Carefully stir a 400 g (13 oz) can of caramel into 400 g (13 oz) Greek yogurt to give a marbled effect. Layer with 3 sliced bananas in 4 glasses and serve sprinkled with 1½ tablespoons grated plain dark chocolate.

 Banana Toffee Trifle

Place 150 g (5 oz) golden syrup, 50 g (2 oz) unsalted butter, 75 g (3 oz) dark muscovado sugar and 50 g (2 oz) caster sugar in a small saucepan over a low heat and heat for 5–6 minutes, stirring from time to time, until the sugars have dissolved. Cook for 2–3 minutes, then gradually stir in 150 ml (5 fl oz) double cream. Leave to cool for 5–6 minutes. Meanwhile, place 150 g (5 oz) amaretti biscuits in a trifle dish and pour over 2–3 tablespoons Amaretto liqueur. Leave to stand for 5 minutes, then gently stir in 3 chopped bananas. Pour over the butterscotch sauce and leave to stand for a further 5–6 minutes. Spoon over 300 ml (½ pint) ready-made custard and chill for 3–4 minutes, then spoon over 275 ml (9 fl oz) whipped cream. Sprinkle over 2 tablespoons grated chocolate to finish.

30 Banana and Honey Flapjacks

Serves 4

oil, for greasing
25 g (1 oz) light muscovado sugar
175 g (6 oz) unsalted butter
1 tablespoon clear honey
1½ tablespoons golden syrup
1 large banana, mashed
300 g (10 oz) rolled oats
75 g (3 oz) dried banana chips,
  roughly broken.

- Lightly grease a 22 cm (8½ inch) square cake tin.

- Place the sugar, butter, honey and golden syrup in a saucepan over a medium heat and heat, stirring occasionally, until the butter has melted and the sugar dissolved. Remove from the heat.

- Stir in the mashed banana and oats and mix well. Spoon one-half of the oat mixture into the prepared tin, sprinkle over the banana chips and top with the remaining oat mixture. Press down and level the top.

- Bake in a preheated oven, 180°C (350°F), Gas Mark 4, for 20–22 minutes until golden.

- Remove from the oven and cut into 12 bars while still hot. Leave to cool in the tin.

 Baked Bananas with Passion Fruit and Honey Place 4 bananas in a preheated oven, 220°C (425°F), Gas Mark 7, or on a barbecue for 10 minutes, until charred. Meanwhile, scoop the pulp out of 4 passion fruit and mix with 450 g (14½ oz) Greek yogurt and the finely grated rind of 1 orange. Split open the bananas, top with a large dollop of the passion fruit yogurt and drizzle with 1 tablespoon clear honey.

 Chocolate- and Honey-Baked Bananas Cut a slit in the skin of 4 bananas along one side. Stick 20 g (¾ oz) chocolate buttons into the cut and pour ½ tablespoon honey over the chocolate. Put each banana on a sheet of foil and seal to make a parcel. Place on a baking sheet and bake in a preheated oven, 200°C (400°F), Gas Mark 6, for 15–18 minutes until the bananas are soft and the chocolate melted. Meanwhile, whisk 300 ml (½ pint) double cream with 2 tablespoons Cointreau and the finely grated rind of 1 orange. Serve the chocolate bananas with a dollop of the orange-flavoured cream.

30 Lemon and Poppyseed Muffins

Serves 4

2 tablespoons clear honey

2 tablespoons poppy seeds

juice of 2 lemons, plus the grated rind of 1 lemon

110 g (3½ oz) unsalted butter, melted

110 g (3½ oz) caster sugar

2 eggs

175 g (6 oz) natural yogurt

350 g (11½ oz) self-raising gluten-free flour

1 teaspoon gluten-free baking powder

½ teaspoon bicarbonate of soda

- Line a 12-hole muffin tin with paper cases.

- Place the honey in a small saucepan over a medium heat and add the poppy seeds, the lemon rind and one-half of the lemon juice. Heat until the honey is melted, then take off the heat and pour into a bowl. Stir in the remaining lemon juice and leave to cool for 1–2 minutes.

- Whisk in the melted butter, sugar, eggs and yogurt.

- Sift the flour, baking powder and bicarbonate of soda into a large bowl and pour in the yogurt mixture. Gently mix together until just combined – do not over mix.

- Divide between the paper muffin cases and bake in a preheated oven, 190°C (375°F), Gas Mark 5, for 15–18 minutes, until golden. Cool on a wire rack.

---

1 **Lemon and Poppyseed Pudding**

Mix together 275 g (9 oz) lemon curd, 500 g (1 lb) crème fraîche, 1 tablespoon poppy seeds and the grated rind of 1 lemon. Stir in 6 crushed amaretti biscuits and spoon into 4 glasses to serve.

2 **Lemon and Poppyseed Scones**

Sift 250 g (8 oz) self-raising gluten-free flour into a bowl with 1 teaspoon gluten-free baking powder. Rub in 50 g (2 oz) unsalted butter until the mixture resembles fine breadcrumbs. Stir in 50 g (2 oz) caster sugar, the grated rind of 1 lemon and 1 tablespoon poppyseeds. Whisk together 1 egg and 150 ml (¼ pint) milk and pour into the flour mixture. Bring the dough together. Using an ice cream scoop, scoop 8–10 mounds of the dough onto a baking sheet. Bake in a preheated oven, 220°C (425°F) Gas Mark 7, for 12–15 minutes until risen and golden. Serve warm with dollops of clotted cream and lemon curd.

GLU-SWEE-RAH

30 Chocolate Orange Shortbread

Serves 4

100 g (3½ oz) unsalted butter,
softened
50 g (2 oz) caster sugar
grated rind of 1 orange
25 g (1 oz) cocoa powder
50 g (2 oz) plain gluten-free flour

- Line a baking sheet with baking paper.

- Cream together the butter, sugar and orange rind until light and fluffy.

- Mix in the cocoa powder and flour and bring together until you have a ball of dough. Cover and chill for 10 minutes.

- Shape the mixture into walnut-sized balls and place on the baking sheet, making sure they are well spaced.

- Bake in a preheated oven, 190°C (375°F), Gas Mark 5, for 5 minutes. Remove the tray from the oven and lightly press down each ball of dough with your finger. Return to the oven and bake for a further 5–7 minutes, until the mixture has started to crisp on top.

- Place on a wire rack to cool completely.

 1 **Chocolate Brownie Orange Pudding**

Place 225 g (7½ oz) chopped plain dark chocolate, 75 g (3 oz) caster sugar and 125 ml (4 fl oz) double cream in a small saucepan over a low heat. Pour in 60 ml (2½ fl oz) hot water and stir until the chocolate has melted and the sauce is hot. Pour over 4 ready-made gluten-free brownies and serve with the segments of 2 oranges, a dollop of crème fraîche and a sprinkling of cocoa powder.

 2 **Chocolate Orange Scones**

Sift 250 g (8 oz) self-raising gluten-free flour into a bowl with 1 teaspoon gluten-free baking powder, the grated rind of 1 orange and 1 tablespoon cocoa powder. Rub in 50 g (2 oz) unsalted butter until the mixture resembles fine breadcrumbs. Stir in 50 g (2 oz) caster sugar. Whisk together 1 egg and 150 ml (¼ pint) milk and pour into the flour mixture. Bring the dough together. Using an ice cream scoop, scoop 8–10 mounds of the dough onto a baking sheet. Bake in a preheated oven, 220°C (425°F), Gas Mark 7, for 12–15 minutes until risen and golden. Serve warm with dollops of clotted cream and grated chocolate.

30 Crispy Cornbread

Serves 4

15 g (½ oz) lard
15 g (½ oz) butter, melted
1 tablespoon vegetable oil
2 spring onions, diced
1 red chilli, deseeded and diced
125 g (4 oz) sweetcorn
150 g (5 oz) polenta or cornmeal
15 g (½ oz) plain gluten-free flour
2 teaspoons gluten-free baking
   powder
1 teaspoon bicarbonate of soda
pinch of salt
2 teaspoons caster sugar
1 egg, beaten
175 ml (6 fl oz) buttermilk

- Grease a 20 cm (8 inch) round cake tin with the lard and place in a preheated oven, 200°C (400°F), Gas Mark 6, to heat.

- Place the butter and oil in a frying pan over a medium heat, add the spring onions, chilli and sweetcorn and cook for 1 minute, then remove from the heat.

- In a large bowl, sift together the polenta or cornmeal, flour, baking powder, bicarbonate of soda, salt and sugar. Make a well in the centre.

- Beat together the egg and buttermilk, then pour into the well and gradually bring the mixture together with a fork.

- Stir in the spring onion mixture.

- Remove the cake tin from the oven and pour in the corn mixture. Return to the oven and bake for 20–23 minutes, until golden.

- Cool on a wire rack and cut into wedges to serve.

Cornbread French Toast

Melt 50 g (2 oz) butter in a large frying pan. Whisk together 3 eggs and 100 ml (3½ fl oz) double cream and dip in 6 thick slices of cornbread. Add to the frying pan and cook for 3–4 minutes on each side, until golden. Meanwhile, cook 12 rashers of unsmoked streaky bacon under a preheated medium grill until crisp. Top the French toast with the bacon and drizzle with maple syrup to serve.

20 Cornbread Muffins

Brush a 12-hole muffin tin with 15 g (½ oz) melted butter. Slice the kernels off 1 large cob of sweetcorn. Melt 25g (1 oz) butter in a saucepan over a medium heat, add the sweetcorn, 1 small diced onion, ½ deseeded and diced red chilli and cook for 2–3 minutes. Sift together 140 g (4¾ oz) plain gluten-free flour, 140 g (4¾ oz) polenta and 2 teaspoons gluten-free baking powder. Stir in 50 g (2 oz) grated Cheddar and a pinch of salt. Whisk together 2 eggs, 50 g (2 oz) melted butter, 300 ml (½ pint) buttermilk and 100 ml (3½ fl oz) milk. Stir the wet ingredients into the dry with the sweetcorn mixture, then divide between the muffin holes. Bake in a preheated oven, 190°C (375°F), Gas Mark 5, for 18–20 minutes until golden and cooked through.

GLU-SWEE-GOM

Chocolate Raspberry Cake

Serves 6-8

oil, for greasing
8 eggs, separated
pinch of salt
400 g (13 oz) plain dark chocolate
150 g (5 oz) unsalted butter
50 g (2 oz) caster sugar
225 g (7½ oz) crème fraîche
grated rind of 1 orange
375 g (12 oz) raspberries
icing sugar, for dusting

- Grease 2 x 18 cm (7 inch) round cake tins.

- Whisk the egg yolks with the salt.

- Melt the chocolate and butter in a heatproof bowl set over a saucepan of gently simmering water. Leave the melted chocolate to cool for 2–3 minutes, then fold in the egg yolks.

- In a grease-free bowl, whisk the egg whites to stiff peaks, then gradually whisk in the sugar.

- Fold the egg whites into the chocolate mixture and pour into the prepared tins. Bake in a preheated oven, 180°C (350°F), Gas Mark 4, for 15 minutes, then remove from the tins and leave to cool.

- Meanwhile, mix together the crème fraîche and orange rind.

- Spread the orange cream over one of the cakes and top with one-half of the raspberries. Place the other cake on top and decorate with the remaining raspberries. Dust with icing sugar to serve.

---

1 **Chocolate Pots with Raspberry Coulis** Place 250 ml (8 fl oz) double cream and 75 g (3 oz) sugar in a pan and bring to the boil, stirring a few times to melt the sugar. Place 200 g (7 oz) chopped plain dark chocolate, 2 egg yolks and the grated rind of 1 orange in a food processor. With the food processor running, pour in the hot cream and process until the chocolate melts. Spoon into 4 glasses and serve with a tablespoon of ready-made raspberry coulis.

 2 **Chocolate Welsh Cakes with Raspberry Jam** Sift together 350 g (11½ oz) plain gluten-free flour, ¼ teaspoon cocoa powder and 1 teaspoon gluten-free baking powder into a bowl. Rub in 150 g (5 oz) butter, until the mixture resembles fine breadcrumbs. Stir in 100 g (3½ oz) caster sugar, 50 g (2 oz) currants, 50 g (2 oz) chocolate chips and the finely grated rind of 1 lemon, then make a well in the centre. Whisk together 2 eggs, 2 teaspoons vegetable oil and 2 teaspoons lemon juice, and whisk into the flour mixture to make a thick batter. Place a lightly oiled frying pan over a medium heat and spoon in mounds of 2–3 teaspoons of the mixture, pressing them down lightly to make cakes. Cook for 2–3 minutes on each side, until lightly golden. Serve spread with raspberry jam and a dollop of crème fraîche.

1⟐ Lemon and Turkish Delight Syllabub

Serves 4

2 tablespoons rose water
50 g (2 oz) caster sugar
400 ml (14 fl oz) whipping cream
2 tablespoons lemon juice
100 g (3½ oz) Turkish Delight,
  diced
grated rind of 1 lemon

- Place the rose water in a large bowl and stir in the sugar until it dissolves.

- Add the cream and whip until soft peaks form. Stir in the lemon juice and Turkish Delight and divide between 4 glasses to serve.

- Serve sprinkled with the lemon rind.

2⟐ Fondant Pudding with Lemon Turkish Delight Syllabub

Melt 125 g (4 oz) unsalted butter with 125 g (4 oz) plain dark chocolate in a heatproof bowl set over a saucepan of gently simmering water. Whisk together 2 eggs, 2 egg yolks and 125 g (4 oz) caster sugar until pale and fluffy. Gently fold in the chocolate mixture, then fold in 2 tablespoons self-raising gluten-free flour. Spoon into 4 lightly oiled and cocoa-dusted moulds and bake in a preheated oven, 200°C (400°F), Gas Mark 6, for 12 minutes. Meanwhile, whisk 150 ml (¼ pint) whipping cream with 25 g (1 oz) caster sugar until soft peaks form, then fold in the rind and juice of ½ lemon and 40 g (1¾ oz) diced Turkish Delight. Chill. Turn out the fondants and serve with the syllabub.

3⟐ Meringue Roulade with Lemon Syllabub and Turkish Delight Filling

Whisk 4 egg whites until very stiff, then whisk in 225 g (7½ oz) caster sugar a tablespoon at a time until the mixture is thick and glossy. Grease a 20 x 30 cm (8 x 12 inch) Swiss roll tin, line it with baking paper and sprinkle with 50 g (2 oz) desiccated coconut. Bake in a preheated oven, 200°C (400°F), Gas Mark 6, for 15–18 minutes until just firm to the touch. Turn out onto a piece of baking paper, then remove the backing paper and loosely roll using the baking paper underneath. Leave to cool for 5 minutes. Mix together the rind and juice of 2 lemons and 4 tablespoons clear honey, stirring until the honey has dissolved. Pour in 600 ml (1 pint) double cream and whisk until soft. Unroll the meringue, spread with the cream and sprinkle over 40 g (1¾ oz) diced Turkish Delight. Gently re-roll to serve.

30 Coconut and Sultana Cookies

Serves 4

125 g (4 oz) unsalted butter, plus extra for greasing

2 tablespoons golden syrup

1 egg, beaten

90 g (3¼ oz) desiccated coconut

50 g (2 oz) rice flour

1 teaspoon gluten-free baking powder

225 g (7½ oz) soft dark brown sugar

325 g (11 oz) sultanas

- Lightly grease 2 baking sheets.

- In a small saucepan, melt together the golden syrup and butter. Leave to cool for 3–4 minutes, then beat in the egg.

- Place the remaining ingredients in a large bowl, pour in the syrup mixture and mix well.

- Place teaspoons of the mixture on the prepared baking sheets (the mixture should yield 12), leaving space for the cookies to spread. Bake in a preheated oven, 180°C (350°F), Gas Mark 4, for 10–15 minutes until golden. Leave to cool on a wire rack.

---

 1 Coconut and Sultana Dessert

Toast 2 tablespoons desiccated coconut under a preheated medium grill for 3–4 minutes until golden. Stir another 2 tablespoons desiccated coconut into 400 g (13 oz) Greek yogurt, then stir in 2 teaspoons clear honey. Spoon one-half of this mixture into 4 glasses. Top with 1 tablespoon sultanas, 1 peeled, stoned and diced mango and 50 g (2 oz) raspberries, then spoon over the remaining yogurt. Sprinkle with the toasted coconut and drizzle with a little more honey to serve.

---

 2 Coconut and Sultana Scones

Sift 250 g (8 oz) self-raising gluten-free flour into a bowl with 1 teaspoon gluten-free baking powder. Stir in 1 tablespoon desiccated coconut. Rub in 50 g (2 oz) unsalted butter until the mixture resembles fine breadcrumbs. Stir in 50 g (2 oz) caster sugar and 50 g (2 oz) sultanas. Whisk together 1 egg and 150 ml (¼ pint) milk and pour into the flour mixture. Bring the dough together. Using an ice cream scoop, scoop 8–10 mounds of the dough onto a baking sheet. Bake in a preheated oven, 220°C (425°F), Gas Mark 7, for 12–15 minutes until risen and golden.

GLU-SWEE-JIC

30 Lemon and Raspberry Cheesecake Tartlets

Serves 4

175 g (6 oz) walnuts
4 dates, pitted
2 tablespoons maple syrup
4 x 7–8 cm (3 inch) shop-bought
    sweet pastry cases
200 g (7 oz) mascarpone cheese
grated rind and juice of 1 lemon
2 tablespoons icing sugar
125 g (4 oz) raspberries

- Place the walnuts in a bowl, cover with cold water and leave to stand for 10 minutes. Drain.

- Place the walnuts, dates and maple syrup in a food processor and blitz until they all come together. Divide the mixture between the pastry cases and press into the base and sides. Chill.

- Meanwhile, mix together the mascarpone, lemon rind and juice and icing sugar. Divide the mixture between the pastry cases. Chill.

- Meanwhile, make a raspberry coulis by pressing the raspberries through a sieve to remove the pips.

- Remove the tartlets from their tins and place each one on a small plate, then top with a drizzle of raspberry coulis.

 Lemon and Raspberry Soda Floats Divide 500 g (1 lb) vanilla ice cream between 4 tall glasses. Pour in enough traditional lemonade to fill the glass. Add 3–4 raspberries to each glass, sprinkle with the grated rind of 1 lemon and serve with long spoons.

 Lemon Soufflés with Raspberry Coulis Mix 1 tablespoon cornflour with a little water, then place in a food processor with 2 chopped bananas, the grated rind of 2 lemons and 1 tablespoon lemon juice and process until nearly smooth. In a grease-free bowl whisk 6 egg whites, gradually adding 150 g (5 oz) caster sugar and 2 teaspoons lemon juice, until smooth soft peaks form. Place the banana mixture into a large bowl and gently fold in the meringue, then divide the mixture between 4 buttered and sugared ramekins. Level the top of each one and make sure the edges are clean. Bake in a preheated oven, 180°C (375°F), Gas Mark 5, for 10–12 minutes until risen and golden. Meanwhile, make a raspberry coulis as above and spoon over the soufflés to serve.

GLU-SWEE-WYN

Index

Page references in *italics*
indicate photographs

Acknowledgements

Recipes by **Joy Skipper**
Executive Editor **Eleanor Maxfield**
Editors **Katy Denny and Alex Stetter**
Art Direction **Tracy Killick and Geoff Fennell** for Tracy Killick Art Direction and Design
Original design concept **www.gradedesign.com**
Designer **Tracy Killick for Tracy Killick Art Direction and Design**
Photographer **William Shaw**
Home Economist **Joy Skipper**
Prop Stylist **Liz Hippisley**
Senior Production Manager **Katherine Hockley**